EXECUTIVE EDITORS
Mike Mifsud, Alan Doan, Jenny Doan,
Sarah Galbraith, David L̶...

...Lauren Dorton, Jennifer Dowling,
Dustin Weant

PATTERN TEAM
Tyler MacBeth, Kimberly Forman, Jessica Toye,
Denise Lane

PROJECT DESIGN TEAM
Jenny Doan, Natalie Earnheart

EDITORS & COPYWRITERS
Camille Maddox, Nichole Spravzoff, David Litherland,
Julie Barber-Arutyunyan

SEWIST TEAM
Jenny Doan, Natalie Earnheart, Carol Henderson,
Janice Richardson

QUILTING & BINDING DEPARTMENT
Janet Yamamoto , Becky Bowen, Glenda Rorabough,
Nikki LaPiana, Amy Turpin, Debbie Elder, Holly
Clevenger, Kristen Cash, Todd Harman, Jessica Paup,
Jan Meek, Linda Frump, Franny Fleming, Rachael
Joyce, Selena Smiley, Nora Clutter, Lyndia Lovell,
Jackie Jones, Roxanna Hinkle, Deloris Burnett,
Bernice Kelley, Darlene Smith

LOCATION CREDIT
Robert (Bob) and Susie Lund, Hamilton, MO
Cameron Historical Society and Depot Museum, C/O
Stan Hendrix, Cameron, MO

PRINTING COORDINATORS
Rob Stoebener, Seann Dwyer

PRINTING SERVICES
Walsworth Print Group
803 South Missouri
Marceline, MO 64658

CONTACT US
Missouri Star Quilt Company
114 N Davis
Hamilton, MO 64644
888-571-1122
info@missouriquiltco.com

content

*Oops! Sometimes we make mistakes.
To find corrections to every issue of Block
go to:* **www.msqc.co/corrections**

hello
from MSQC

What is it about fall we love so much? Is it the blissful break from summer's heat? Is it the fresh harvest of fruits and vegetables that we spent all summer tending? Is it the anticipation of upcoming holidays? Or is it something more? As I watch leaves pile up without the desire to rake them away, I realize that what I love so much about this season is letting go. I let go of carefully tending my yard. I slow down and go inward, preparing for the winter, allowing myself to curl up with a well-worn quilt and let time pass by slowly. I try to let go of unnecessary constraints on my time and energy and focus on the things that matter most.

Letting go is also about giving ourselves the freedom to say yes to new things. There are always those things that must be done, but what about the things we choose to do? Choosing to allow creativity into each day gives me a fresh perspective and a greater desire to do the things I must do. It's incredible how energized I feel after a walk, observing fall colors, and bringing them into my fabric and design choices. Because I make so many quilts, taking these moments to pause makes it less of a chore and more of a time to reflect. I can let go and let creativity flow. May this season fill you with inspiration and the desire to create beautiful things. Start small and just see what happens!

JENNY DOAN
MISSOURI STAR QUILT CO.

TRY OUR APP

It's easy to keep up on every issue of BLOCK magazine. Access it from all your devices. And when you subscribe to BLOCK, it's free with your subscription! For the app, search BLOCK magazine in the app store. Available for both Apple and Android.

For the tutorial and everything you need to make this quilt visit:

www.msqc.co/blockfall19

square knot

Here in the Midwest, we eat a lot of corn! Cornbread, corn-on-the-cob, popcorn, corn flakes, and sometimes even hominy and grits are on nearly every menu. It gets to the point that we kind of take corn for granted. But corn wasn't always the sweet, yellow kernels we know and love today. Here are some fascinating facts about the crops we grow.

Corn has been a staple crop in the Americas since the earliest days of farming. Ancient civilizations were growing corn in Central America over ten thousand years ago! But, the corn they were growing didn't look anything like the corn you get at the grocery store today; it looked more like wheat! Instead of dozens of rows of yellow kernels, there was one small row of green seeds with hard shells covering the tiny nutritious bits of the plant.

Archaeologists think that early corn wasn't very tasty, and took a long time to grow, only to produce a few kernels that needed a lot of work to get them out of the shells. The early Native Americans must have agreed because, over time, the plants were mixed with other types of crops, and the best ones kept being selected by the farmers until we ended up with the lovely vegetable we know today, with full, plump, non-shelled kernels. Before too long, Native Americans were growing corn from the Pacific Northwest to the Great Plains, and from the Aztec Empire in modern-day Mexico to the mountaintops of the Andes. Even this corn was different from today's, though; it wasn't until the 19th century that farmers produced all-yellow corn!

And it wasn't just corn that went through this transformation, either; just about every fruit or vegetable you eat today has been tweaked and improved over hundreds of years. There's paintings of watermelons from over 400 years ago that show a fruit full of large, black seeds and just a tiny bit of pink flesh inside a rind over an inch thick. Back then, this would have been a delicacy; now, you can pop down to the grocery store and pick

up a watermelon filled to the brim with sweet red fruity goodness, and none of the seeds.

Not all of the changes were just to make the plants better at their jobs, though. Back in the medieval ages, carrots used to come in any color you could imagine. It wasn't until the 1600s that farmers in the Netherlands wanted to celebrate the coronation of William of Orange, a Dutch prince who became the King of England! Nowadays, it's hard to find a carrot that's not old William III's favorite color.

All of the work that's gone into these tasty crops by generations of farmers shouldn't be taken for granted. So, the next time you bite into some sweet corn-on-the-cob, a crunchy orange carrot, or a juicy seedless watermelon, remember to thank all those farmers for the tasty treat!

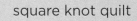

materials

QUILT SIZE
72" x 72"

BLOCK SIZE
8" finished

QUILT TOP
1 roll 2½" print strips
1 roll 2½" background strips

INNER BORDER
¼ yard - matching the 2½"
background strips

OUTER BORDER
1½ yards

BINDING
¾ yard

BACKING
4½ yards - vertical seam(s)

SAMPLE QUILT
Golden Days by Fancy Pants Designs
for Riley Blake

1 cut

From the 2½" print strips:

- Choose (24) 2½" strips. Cut
  (8) 2½" x 4½" rectangles from
  each strip. Keep matching
  rectangles together in sets of 4.

- Take (12) 2½" strips. Cut (16)
  2½" squares from each strip. Keep
  matching squares together in sets
  of 4.

- Select (1) 2½" strip and cut (4)
  2½" x 4½" rectangles and (4)
  2½" squares. Add these to
  the previously cut rectangles
  and squares for a **total of 196**
  print rectangles and a **total of
  196** print squares.

Set the 3 remaining strips aside for
another project.

From the 2½" background strips:

- Choose (24) 2½" strips. Cut (8)
  2½" x 4½" rectangles from
  each strip.

- Take (12) 2½" strips. Cut (16)
  2½" squares from each strip.

- Select (1) 2½" strip and cut
  (4) 2½" x 4½" rectangles and
  (4) 2½" squares. Add these to the
  previously cut rectangles
  and squares for a **total of 196**
  background rectangles and a
  total of 196 background squares.
  Set the 3 remaining strips aside
  for the inner border.

2A

2B

2C

2D

3A

3B

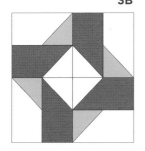

From the background fabric, cut (3) 2½" strips across the width of the fabric. Add these to the remaining (3) 2½" background strips and set all 6 strips aside for the inner border.

2 sew

Draw a diagonal line, corner to corner, on the back side of each 2½" square.

Take a 2½" x 4½" print rectangle and lay a 2½" background square on top, right sides together. Line up the left edges as shown and sew on the diagonal line. **2A**

Trim away excess, leaving a ¼" seam allowance. Open and press the seam allowance toward the triangle. Repeat for a **total of 196** A Units. **2B**

Take a 2½" x 4½" background rectangle and lay a 2½" print square on top, right sides together. Line up the left edges as shown and sew on the diagonal line. **2C**

Trim away excess, leaving a ¼" seam allowance. Open and press the seam allowance toward the triangle. Repeat for a **total of 196** B Units. **2D**

3 block construction

Turning the A Units and B Units so that the triangles are on the left, take 1 B Unit and lay 1 A Unit on top, right sides together. Sew along the top using a ¼" seam allowance. Open and press toward darker fabric. Repeat for 3 additional matching AB units. **3A**

Arrange the 4 matching units as shown. Sew the top 2 units together and press the seam to the left. Sew the bottom 2 units together and press the seam to the right. Nest the seams and sew the units as shown to complete the block. **Make 49. 3B**

Block Size: 8" finished

4 arrange & sew

Lay out your blocks in **7 rows** of **7 blocks** each. Sew the blocks together in rows. Press the seam allowances of all odd rows to the left and all even rows to the right. Nest the seams and sew the rows together.

5 inner border

Sew the remaining (6) 2½" background strips end-to-end to make 1 long strip. Trim the inner borders from this strip.

Refer to Borders (pg. 102) in the Construction Basics to measure and cut the borders. The strips are approximately 56½" for the sides and approximately 60½" for the top and bottom.

6 outer border

From the outer border fabric, cut (7) 6½" strips across the width of the fabric. Sew the strips together end-to-end to make 1 long strip. Trim the outer borders from this strip.

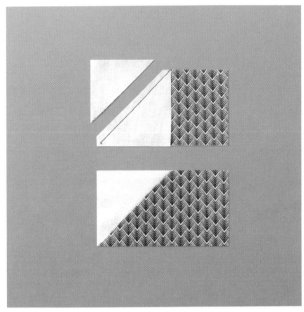

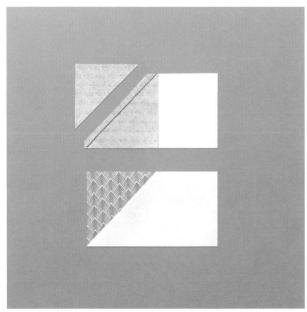

1 Lay a 2½″ background square on top of a 2½″ x 4½″ print rectangle, right sides together. Line up the left edges as shown and sew on the marked diagonal line. Trim away the excess, leaving a ¼″ seam allowance. Open and press the seam allowance toward the triangle. Repeat for a total of 196 A Units.

2 Lay a 2½″ print square on top of 2½″ x 4½″ background rectangle, right sides together. Line up the left edges as shown and sew on the marked diagonal line. Trim away excess, leaving a ¼″ seam allowance. Open and press the seam allowance toward the triangle. Repeat for a total of 196 B Units.

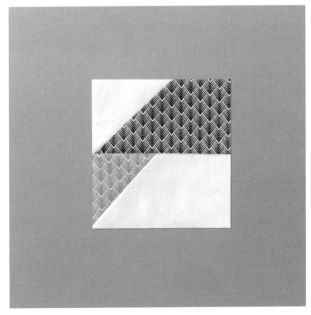

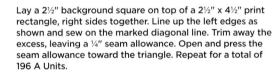

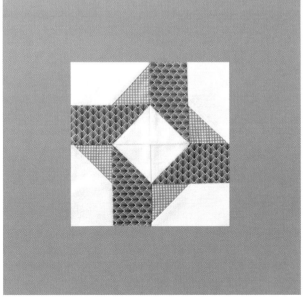

3 Taking 1 B Unit with a print triangle on the left, lay 1 A Unit on top, triangle on the left, right sides together. Sew along the top using a ¼″ seam allowance. Open and press toward the darker fabric.

4 Arrange 4 matching units. Sew the top 2 units together, pressing the seam to the left. Sew the bottom 2 units together, pressing the seam to the right. Nest the seams and sew the units to complete the block. Make 49.

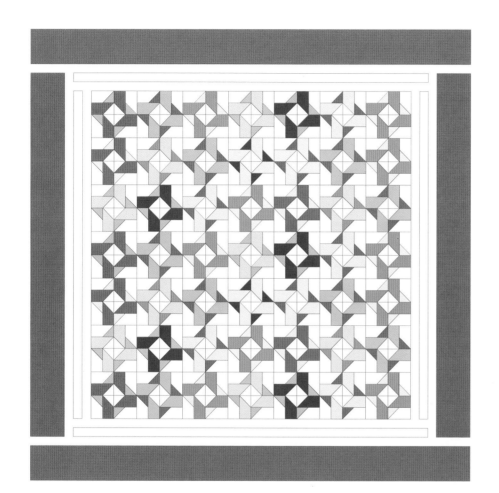

Refer to Borders (pg. 102) in the Construction Basics to measure and cut the borders. The strips are approximately 60½″ for the sides and approximately 72½″ for the top and bottom.

7 quilt & bind

Layer the quilt with batting and backing and quilt. After the quilting is complete, square up the quilt and trim away all excess batting and backing. Add binding to complete the quilt. See Construction Basics (pg. 102) for binding instructions.

fancy *flight*

"Autumn is a second spring when every leaf is a flower."
-Albert Camus

After months of hot, sticky weather, fall arrives in Hamilton like a breath of fresh air. Brisk mornings give way to sun-soaked afternoons. The atmosphere is light and crisp, and the leaves burst into a rainbow of red and gold. Those leaves! That transformation from green to fire is nothing short of magic. I know I'm not alone in my admiration, and I've just learned there is a name for people like us: leaf peepers!

Serious leaf peepers go to great lengths to enjoy those brilliant fall colors. Some take organized "foliage tours" to New England, the upper Midwest, and even Japan. The trick is timing it just right. Like a brilliant sunset, the colors of fall are far too fleeting. Too early and the leaves are still green. Too late and they've faded and fallen. But when you catch them at their peak, it's a sensory delight. With every step, leaves crunch underfoot. A rich, earthy aroma fills the air. And everywhere you look: color!

My friend Annette keeps a small framed leaf on the bookshelf in her living room. "I've had it since my very first date with Andrew," she explained. "Having grown up in Florida, he had never experienced fall as we do here. So when the leaves started to turn, he asked me to accompany him to my favorite wooded trail.

"We meandered through the trees, chatting, and feeling a little bit twitterpated. As we rounded the bend, I stopped in my tracks and grabbed Andrew's hand. There, directly in front of us was a young sugar maple. It resembled a teenager who had just experienced a growth spurt: tall, slender, and a bit gangly.

"Scarlet red leaves were spread around the base of its skinny trunk like a Christmas tree skirt. Even more remarkable than the brilliance of their color was the light dusting of sparkle that covered each and every crimson leaf. Certainly there is some scientific explanation, but to

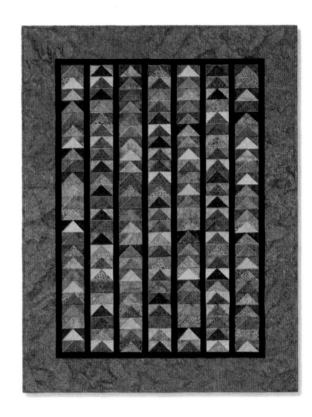

me, those shimmering red leaves seemed as enchanted as Cinderella's pumpkin carriage! I bent down and picked up a leaf. It was small, less than two inches across, but perfectly formed. Andrew was still holding my hand. In fact, he held it all the way back to the car.

"At home, I wrote a love-drunk entry in my journal and pressed the little leaf between the pages. That was chapter one in our story. Our happily ever after has lasted almost four decades. We have wandered the woods together every autumn, searching for the prettiest leaves, but nothing has ever come close to that first sparkly red maple."

materials

QUILT SIZE
47" x 61"

BLOCK SIZE
4" x 2" finished

QUILT TOP
1 roll 2½" print strips*
¾ yard sashing fabric
 - includes inner border

OUTER BORDER
1 yard

BINDING
½ yard

BACKING
3¼ yards - horizontal seam(s)

Strips need to be 42" of usable width. If your fabric is less than 42" of usable width, add an additional ¼ yard of a coordinating print fabric and cut (2) 2½" strips and add them to your roll.

SAMPLE QUILT
Islander Batik by Kathy Engle for Island Batik Fabrics

1 cut & sort

From the sashing fabric, cut (12) 1½" strips across the width of the fabric. Set aside.

Sort the 2½" print strips into 20 dark strips and 20 light strips.

Taking 8 dark 2½" print strips, cut (9) 2½" x 4½" rectangles from each strip. You will need 72 dark rectangles.

From 12 dark 2½" print strips, cut (16) 2½" squares from each strip. You will need 192 dark squares.

Taking 11 light print 2½" strips, cut (9) 2½" x 4½" rectangles from each strip.

You will need 96 light rectangles. Set aside 3 rectangles for another project.

From 9 light 2½" print strips, cut (16) 2½" squares from each strip. You will need 144 light squares.

On the wrong side of each square, draw a diagonal line from 1 corner to the other.

2 sew

Take a 4½" rectangle from the light stack and lay a 2½" square from the dark stack on top, right sides together. Line up the edges and sew on the

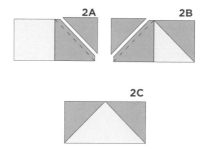

2A 2B

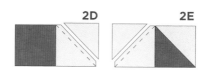

2C

2D 2E

2F

3A 3B

diagonal line. Trim away excess, leaving a ¼″ seam allowance. Open and press the seam allowance toward the outside edge. **2A**

Take the second matching 2½″ square from the dark stack and lay on the opposing side of the 4½″ rectangle, right sides together. Making sure the diagonal is turned the opposite direction, line up the edges, and sew on the diagonal line. Trim away the excess, leaving a ¼″ seam allowance. Open and press the seams toward the outer edge. **Make 96** of Block A. **2B 2C**

Block Size: 4″ x 2″ finished

Take a 4½″ rectangle from the dark stack, and lay a 2½″ square from the light stack on top, right sides together. Line up edges and sew on diagonal line. Trim away excess, leaving a ¼″ seam allowance. Open and press the seam allowance toward the outer edge. **2D**

Take the second matching 2½″ square from the light stack and lay on the opposing side of the 4½″ rectangle, right sides together.

Making sure the diagonal line is turned the opposite direction of the first square, line up the edges, and sew on the diagonal line. Trim away excess, leaving a

¼″ seam allowance. Open and press seam allowance toward outer edge. **Make 72** of Block B. **2E 2F**

Block Size: 4″ x 2″ finished

3 arrange & sew

This quilt will be assembled in vertical rows. It is made up of **7 rows** of **24 blocks.** Select 24 A Blocks and arrange them in a vertical row with the flying geese pointed upwards. Sew the blocks together and press seams toward the bottom. **Make 4. 3A**

Select 24 B Blocks and arrange them in a vertical row with the flying geese pointed upwards. Sew the blocks together and press seams toward the bottom. **Make 3. 3B**

4 sashing

Measure each vertical row, and trim if needed so that all rows are the same length, approximately 48½″ long. Taking the (12) 1½″ strips, sew the strips end-to-end to create 1 long strip.

From the long 1½″ strip, cut 6 sashing strips to the length of your vertical rows. Set aside the remaining strip for the inner border. Refer to the diagram on page 21 to arrange the strips and vertical rows. Notice that all odd vertical rows are made

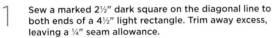

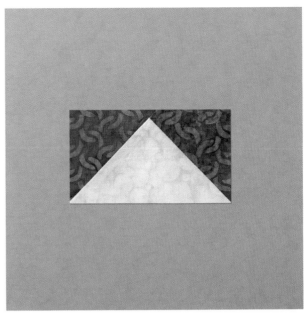

1 Sew a marked 2½″ dark square on the diagonal line to both ends of a 4½″ light rectangle. Trim away excess, leaving a ¼″ seam allowance.

2 Open and press the seams toward the outside edges.

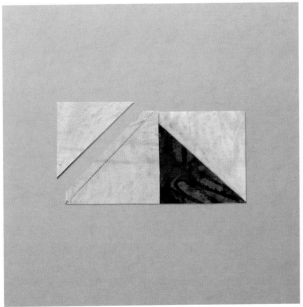

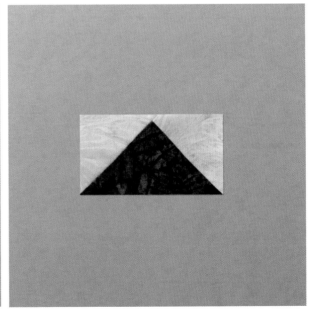

3 Sew a marked 2½″ light square on the diagonal line to both ends of a 4½″ dark rectangle. Trim away excess, leaving a ¼″ seam allowance.

4 Open and press the seams toward outside edges.

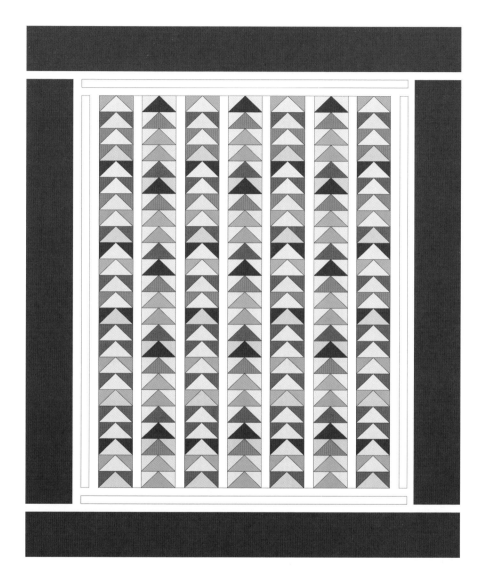

of A Blocks, and all even vertical rows are made of B Blocks. With all triangles pointing up, sew a sashing strip between each vertical row.

5 inner border

Use the remainder of the 1½" strip you set aside earlier to trim the inner borders.

Refer to Borders (pg. 102) in the Construction Basics to measure and cut the borders. The strips are approximately 48½" for the sides and approximately 36½" for the top and bottom.

6 outer border

From the outer border fabric, cut (5) 6" strips across the width of the fabric. Sew the strips together end-to-end to make 1 long strip. Trim the borders from this strip.

Refer to Borders (pg. 102) in the Construction Basics to measure and cut the borders. The strips are approximately 50½" for the sides and approximately 47½" for the top and bottom.

7 quilt & bind

Layer the quilt with batting and backing and quilt. After the quilting is complete, square up the quilt and trim away all excess batting and backing. Add binding to complete the quilt. See Construction Basics (pg. 102) for binding instructions.

For the tutorial and everything
you need to make this quilt visit:
www.msqc.co/blockfall19

mini rhombus
table runner

When summer vacation ends, I start to get giddy about school supplies. I know, I know, it's been a few years since I was in school. It's actually been a few years since my kids were in school! Even so, those perfect yellow pencils and boxes of sharp-tipped crayons just send my heart aflutter!

The pencil is an unsung hero, you know. No ink leaks. No batteries. Forgiving and erasable. Cheap, dependable, practically perfect in every way. Before the pencil, our poor ancestors were writing on cave walls with ash, carving into turtle shells, and scratching messages on wax tablets. But in 16th century England, a discovery was made that would change writing forever.

Legend has it that in 1565, a tree fell over in Borrowdale, England, revealing a layer of rock with dark grey veins. It was graphite. Locals discovered that graphite was easy to saw into rods, and those rods made fantastic marks—marks that were erasable! The only trouble was, it was kind of soft and broke easily. At first, they wrapped the rods in string or leather. Soon, a wooden casing was developed and the pencil was born. But ... they weren't yellow!

Early pencils were manufactured without paint in order to show off the quality of wood. But, at the 1889 Exposition Universelle in Paris, the Hardtmuth Pencil company unveiled their brand new luxury pencil. It was made with Chinese graphite, reportedly the best in the world. And to distinguish these pencils as superior, they were painted bright yellow, the royal color of China.

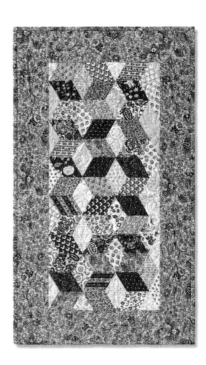

Boy, oh, boy, was that a successful marketing ploy! Before long, everyone was painting their pencils yellow to prove their quality! (Just imagine, if Hardtmuth had chosen lilac to market their luxury pencils, we'd all be writing with purple!)

The next time you pull out your trusty number two pencil to jot down the grocery list or sketch a new quilt design, take a moment to appreciate the amazing invention you hold in your hand. After hundreds of years and mountains of technology, there's nothing quite as reliable as a simple yellow pencil!

Writing Roll Up

PROJECT SIZE: 5¾" x 7¾"

SAMPLE PROJECT

I Dream in Color – Crayons and
Rainbows by Crayola for Riley Blake

SUPPLY LIST

(2) 12" x 16" rectangles of print fabric –
   inner & outer panels

(1) 1¼" x 18" rectangle – strap

(1) 12" x 6" rectangle – pocket

(1) 11½" x 15½" rectangle of fusible fleece

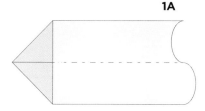

1A

1B

1 make the strap

Fold the strap in half lengthwise, wrong sides together. Press. Open gently without removing the center crease. Fold the ends in at a 45˚ angle to meet the center crease. Press. Fold the raw edges in to meet at the center crease. **1A 1B**

Refold the strap to enclose the raw edges within the strap and press. Topstitch to finish it, backstitching at both ends.

2 make the outer panel

Align the short sides of the outer panel and fold in half. Press a crease into the fabric. Fold it in half the other way and press a crease.

Measure 3⅞" from the top folded edge along the folded spine of the pencil case and make a mark. Unfold. Fold the strap in half to locate the center. Match the center of the strap to the mark you made on the outer panel and topstitch in place. Set aside for now. **2A 2B**

3 make the inner panel

Fold the top edge of the pocket down ¼" and press. Fold over ¼" again and press. Topstitch across the folded edge. Fold the pocket in half and press to mark the center. Open.

Apply the fusible fleece to the wrong side of the inner panel following the manufacturer's instructions. Lay the pocket on top of the inner panel with the right sides of both pieces facing up and the bottom edges aligned. Baste in place with an ⅛" seam allowance.

Start at the bottom edge of the pocket and sew up the center line you marked with a crease, backstitching at the top of the pocket. Mark parallel lines in 1" increments in either direction as needed. Sew along the marked lines. **3A**

4 assemble the project

Place the outer panel on top of the inner panel, right sides together. Be sure the top of both pieces are aligned and the strap is tucked well within the seam allowance. Pin in place if desired. Sew around all 4 sides with a ¼" seam allowance leaving a 3-4" opening.

Trim the corners and turn the project right side out. Press. Topstitch around the perimeter to finish.

2A

fold

3⅞"

fold

mark

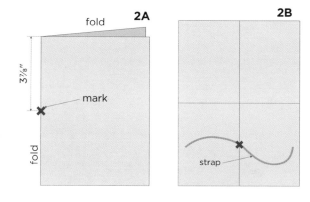

2B

strap

3A

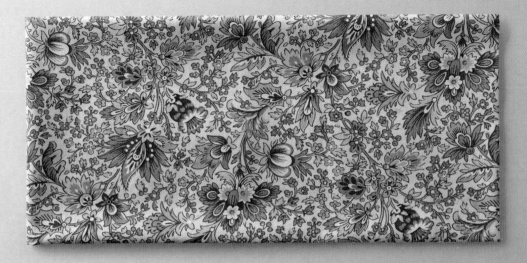

materials

TABLE RUNNER
33" x 18½"

TABLE RUNNER TOP
1 package 5" print squares

BORDER
½ yard

BINDING
¼ yard

BACKING
¾ yard

OTHER
Missouri Star Mini Rhombus Template

SAMPLE QUILT
Chafarcani by French General
for Moda Fabrics

1 cut

Select (20) 5" dark squares from
your package. Cut each selected dark
square in half to yield (2) 2½" x 5"
rectangles. Subcut 39 rhombuses from
the rectangles using the template.
Set the remaining rectangle aside for
another project.

Select (17) 5" light squares from your
package and set the remaining 5"
squares aside for another project. Cut
each selected light square in half to
yield (2) 2½" x 5" rectangles. Use the
template again to subcut 2 triangles
from each of the rectangles. A **total
of 65** triangles are needed. Keep the

matching triangles together. Set the
remaining rectangle aside for another
project.

2 arrange & sew

This table runner is arranged so 2
matching triangles form the top of a
tumbling block. It's important to lay out
the whole table runner before sewing
because the pieces must match the
vertical row next to it.

Begin laying out the table runner along
the bottom horizontal row. This row is
made up of 13 triangles. The first triangle
on the left side of this row points

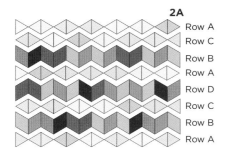

2A

Row A
Row C
Row B
Row A
Row D
Row C
Row B
Row A

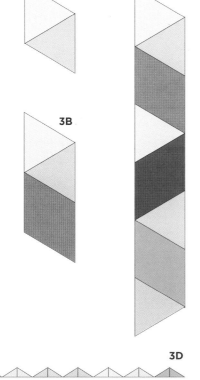

3A

3C

3B

3D

toward the right. Beginning with the second triangle in this row, 2 triangles of matching fabric are set next to each other and point in opposite directions. This is repeated for the remaining triangles in the row. Let's call this Row A for clarity. **2A**

Lay out the next horizontal row up from the bottom. This row is a made up of 13 rhombuses that alternate orientation. Let's call this Row B for clarity.

Next add a third horizontal row from the bottom. This row is made up of 13 triangles and is the opposite orientation of Row A. Let's call this Row C for clarity.

Next add another row of rhombuses. These are oriented opposite of Row B. Let's call this Row D for clarity.

Add another row just like Row A next. Then add another Row B followed by a Row C, and finish it off with another Row A.

3 sew

From now on, we are going to work in vertical rows for constructing this table runner. Begin with the triangle on the left side of the top horizontal row of the table runner and sew it to the triangle

that is directly below it. Press the seam toward the bottom. **3A**

Sew the rhombus that is next in the vertical row to the bottom of the second triangle. Press the seam toward the bottom. **3B**

Continue sewing the triangles and rhombuses to the bottom in the order that they are laid out until you have sewn the entire vertical row. Press all of the seams in this vertical row toward the bottom. **3C**

Sew the rest of the vertical rows together in the same manner, pressing all of the seams in the odd-numbered rows toward the bottom and all of the seams in the even-numbered rows toward the top.

Nest the seams and sew the vertical rows together.

After the rows are sewn together, trim the top and bottom edges of the table runner. Be sure to leave a ¼" seam allowance as you trim. **3D**

4 border

Cut (3) 4" strips across the width of the fabric. Sew the strips together end-to-end to make 1 long strip. Trim the borders from this strip.

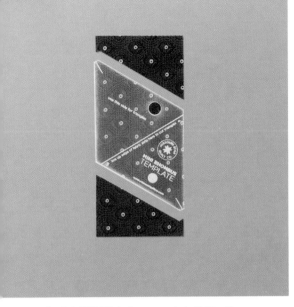

1 Cut (20) 5" dark squares in half. Use the template to subcut a rhombus from 39 of the rectangles and set the remaining rectangle aside.

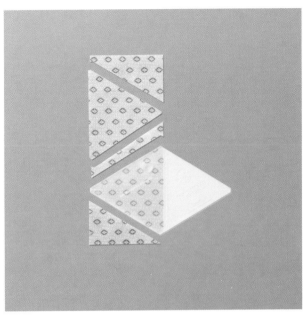

2 Cut (17) 5" light squares in half. Subcut each rectangle again using the template to yield 2 triangles. A total of 65 triangles are needed.

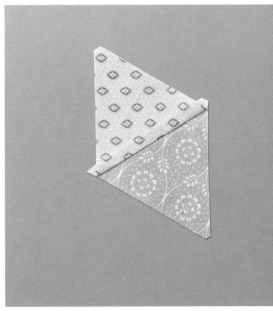

3 After arranging all of the pieces in your table runner, pick up the 2 triangles at the top of the first vertical row and sew them together. Press the seam toward the bottom.

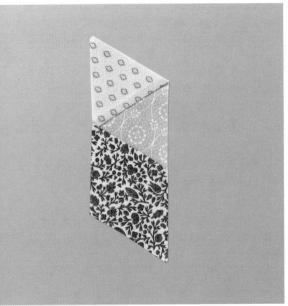

4 Sew the rhombus that is next in the first vertical row to the lower triangle. Press the seam toward the rhombus.

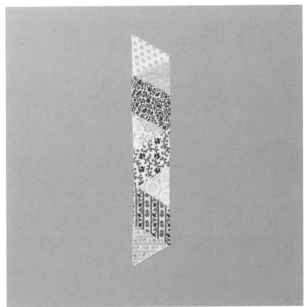

5 Continue adding the triangles and rhombuses until you reach the bottom of the vertical row. Press the seam towards the bottom after sewing each piece.

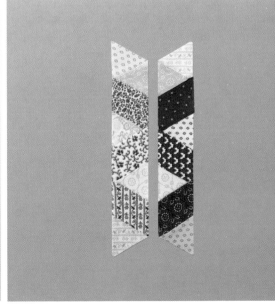

6 Sew the rest of the pieces together to form the vertical rows. Pick up the first and second vertical row and sew them together to start building the center of your table runner.

Refer to Borders (pg. 102) in the Construction Basics to measure and cut the borders. The strips are approximately 12″ for the sides and approximately 33½″ for the top and bottom.

5 quilt & bind

Layer the table runner with batting and backing and quilt. After the quilting is complete, square up the table runner and trim away all excess batting and backing. Add binding to complete the project. See Construction Basics (pg. 102) for binding instructions.

castle *wall*

Have you ever participated in a quilting bee? It calls to mind a group of hardworking pioneers, gathered around a wooden frame with a quilt stretched over it, carefully hand stitching intricate designs as they exchanged small-town gossip and chatted about the cares of the day. It became more than a way of creating a quilt more quickly, it was a social event that brought people together.

Bees are a traditional symbol for working together and although one little worker bee can only make about $\frac{1}{12}$ of a teaspoon of honey in her lifetime, a hive of 10,000 to 60,000 bees can make 20 to 60 pounds of honey in a year! Likewise, at an old-fashioned quilting bee makers from an entire community could hand stitch a quilt in a day or less. What might have taken one person months or years to finish could be completed quickly with the help of others.

Beyond the necessity of finishing a quilt, bees were a social event. As the quilt was completed by the women, the men worked at their separate tasks. By the end of the afternoon, they met back together for dinner, playing games, and dancing into the night. Often, unmarried men and women would meet at quilting bees. Sometimes, a game would be played with the

For the tutorial and everything you need to make this quilt visit:
www.msqc.co/blockfall19

finished quilt called "Cat Shaking" or "The Cat in the Quilt." An unsuspecting cat would be placed in the center of a quilt that was held all along the edges by the young men and ladies. They would then toss the cat into the air on the quilt and whomever the cat jumped at first would be the next to marry!

Nowadays, we don't seem to gather as often to create quilts together, but there are so many ways in our modern world to feel the help and support of others. Many quilters still meet weekly or monthly in guilds, quilting bees, or sew-ins to work together, but quite a few are staying connected digitally too. Online quilting bees, sew-a-longs, and social media make it easy to gather ideas from a group of like-minded quilters and share our creations. Some quilters even send along blocks to each other that eventually end up as a finished quilt. Quilt shows often have a category for group or bee quilts and the results are incredible! The efforts of clever quilters with nimble minds and fingers combine beautifully in these ingenious quilts. Search the hashtag #beesewcial on Instagram and see for yourself!

Our ability to connect with each other is no longer constrained by our physical location. Quilting bees once brought together small communities, but now quilting is a global community! We can meet and become inspired by quilters around the world. Never hesitate to reach out and share, you never know who you might touch. Show us your unique creations by posting on our Facebook page or on Instagram with the hashtag **#msqcshowandtell**.

materials

QUILT SIZE
72½" x 84½"

BLOCK SIZE
4½", 9½" x 4½", and 14½" x 19½" finished

QUILT TOP
1 panel
1 package 10" print squares
¼ yard contrasting fabric

BORDER
1½ yards

BINDING
¾ yard

BACKING
5¼ yards - vertical seam(s)
   or 2¾ yards of 108" wide

SAMPLE QUILT
Bramble by Gingiber for Moda Fabrics

1 cut

Cut the 4 sections of the panel apart on the printed lines. These panel rectangles each measure approximately 15" x 20".

Note: If your panel rectangles are a different size than what we have used, you may need to adjust the length of your borders and the size to cut the contrasting fabric rectangles.

From each print square, cut (2) 10" x 5" rectangles. Subcut 6 rectangles in half to yield a **total of (12)** 5" squares.

From the contrasting fabric, cut a 2¼" strip across the width of the fabric. Subcut the strip into (2) 2¼" x 20" rectangles. **1A 1B**

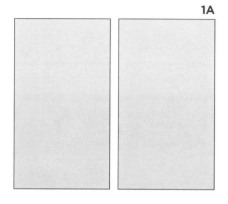

1A

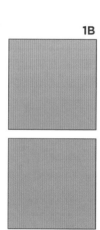

1B

2 arrange & sew

Lay out the quilt center as shown in the diagram on page 39. The first row is made up of a 5″ square followed by (6) 10″ x 5″ rectangles. The second row is made up of (6) 10″ x 5″ rectangles followed by a 5″ square. These rows are alternated throughout the quilt center with the exception of the row that features the panel pieces. That row is made up of the 4 panel rectangles sewn together and a 2¼″ x 20″ rectangle sewn to either end of the row. Sew the squares and rectangles together into rows. Press the seams of the odd-numbered rows to the right and the even-numbered rows to the left. **2A**

Nest the seams and sew the rows together to complete the quilt center.

3 border

Cut (8) 6″ strips across the width of the fabric. Sew the strips together end-to-end to make 1 long strip. Trim the borders from this strip.

Refer to Borders (pg. 102) in the Construction Basics to measure and cut the borders. The strips are approximately 74″ for the sides and approximately 73″ for the top and the bottom.

4 quilt & bind

Layer the quilt with batting and backing and quilt. After the quilting is complete, square up the quilt and trim away all excess batting and backing. Add binding to complete the quilt. See Construction Basics (pg. 102) for binding instructions.

2A

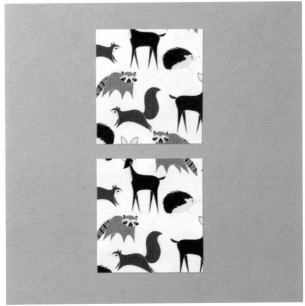

1   Cut each print square in half. Each square will yield 2 rectangles.

2   Select 6 rectangles and subcut them in half to yield 2 squares from each rectangle.

3   Make a row by sewing 1 square to 6 rectangles. Make another row by sewing 6 rectangles and ending with a square. Make an additional 5 rows of each type and sew them together as shown in the diagram on the opposite page.

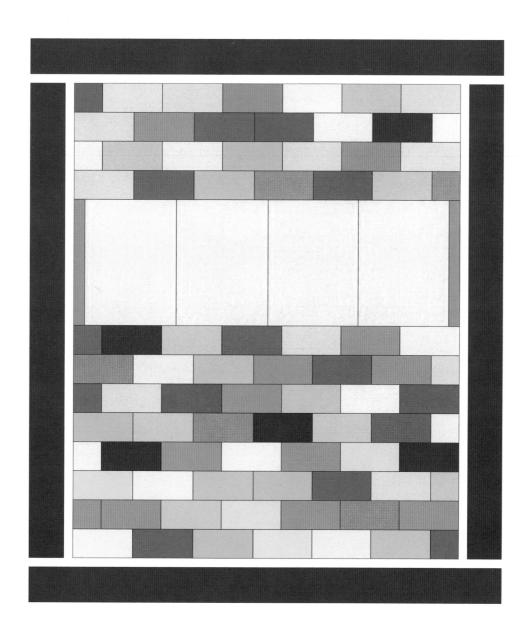

For the tutorial and everything you need to make this quilt visit:
www.msqc.co/blockfall19

four
square

Fun fact: 165 years ago, Hamilton, Missouri did not exist. It's true! This area was nothing more than an unsettled prairie owned by the United States Government. But the railroad was on its way, so in 1854, the Hamilton Town Company was created to prepare the land. Soon, there was one home built. Then there were twenty-five. A general store/post office popped up. The town began to take shape.

On Valentine's Day in 1859, the Hannibal & St. Joseph Railroad was completed, and the first train arrived in Hamilton that very same day. In the years that followed, Hamilton flourished with two banks, two hotels, two newspapers, and a population of 1,800 people. There were flour mills, grain elevators, and even a coal mining company. The wild prairie had been transformed into a vibrant community, all because of the railroad!

A lot has changed since those days, though the town has remained small and quaint. Our downtown streets are still lined with beautiful historic buildings, many of which have been brought back to life as quilt shops.

As you walk through town, you'll see a beautiful mural on the north side of our main quilt shop. It is a depiction of the Hamilton train depot as it must have appeared in the olden days. A big black train engine is steaming along the tracks, and it almost feels like you could step right into the painting and enter the world of 19th century Hamilton.

Can you imagine what it would have been like to board that train for the very first time, to race across the untouched prairie at speeds never before dreamed possible?

The railroad has long since disappeared from our local landscape, but its influence can be felt in every corner of our little town. So while I love to zip down the freeway or hop on an easy flight to some far-off destination, I'll always have a soft spot for the clickety-clack of a journey on the rails.

materials

QUILT SIZE
77" x 92½"

BLOCK SIZE
13½" finished

QUILT TOP
2 packages 5" print squares
½ yard black solid
2¾ yards white solid*
¼ yard coordinating print**

BORDER
1¾ yards

BINDING
¾ yard

BACKING
5¾ yards - vertical seams
    or 3 yards of 108" width

The fabric you select needs to have a minimum of 42" of usable width.
**Note: There is enough backing fabric included that you can cut (2) 2½" strips from the backing fabric to use for the coordinating print if desired.

SAMPLE QUILT
Seasons by Jason Yenter for In The Beginning Fabrics

1 cut

From the black fabric, cut (10) 1½" strips across the width of the fabric.

From the white fabric, cut:

*   (10) 4" strips across the width of the fabric and set them aside for the moment.

*   (3) 5" strips across the width of the fabric. Subcut the strips into 5" squares. Each strip will yield 8 squares and a **total of 20** are needed. Set 4 of the squares aside for another project.

2 sew

Lay a black strip atop a white strip with the long edges aligned on 1 side and right sides facing. Sew the strips together lengthwise. Press toward the darker fabric. **Make 10. 2A**

Cut 5" segments across the width of the strip sets. Each strip set will yield 8 segments and a **total of 80** are needed. **2B**

2A

2B

3 construct the blocks

Select 4 print squares from your package, 1 white square, and 4 of the black and white segments cut from the strip. Arrange the pieces in 3 rows of 3 as shown. Sew the pieces together in rows. Press the seams of the top and bottom rows to the right. Press the seams of the middle row to the left. **3A**

Nest the seams and sew the rows together to complete the block. Press. **Make 20. 3B**

Block Size: 13½" finished

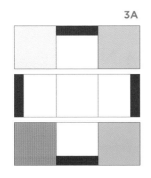

3A

4 make horizontal sashing strips

From the white fabric, cut (17) 2½" strips across the width of the fabric. Subcut the strips into 2½" x 14" rectangles. Each strip will yield 3 rectangles and a **total of 49** rectangles are needed.

From the coordinating print, cut (2) 2½" strips across the width of the fabric. Subcut the strips into 2½" squares. Each strip will yield 16 squares and a **total of 30** are needed.

Sew a 2½" square to the end of (4) 2½" x 14" rectangles. Sew another 2½" square to the opposite end of 1 of the units. Sew all of the units together to form a row making sure to alternate between

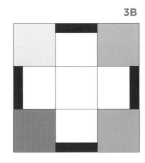

3B

squares and rectangles. Press all of the seams toward the rectangles. **Make 6. 4A**

5 arrange & sew

Lay out the blocks in **5 rows** with each row being made up of **4 blocks**. As you make each row, sew a 2½" x 14" sashing rectangle between each block and to the beginning and end of the row. Press the seam allowances toward the sashing rectangles.

Sew the rows together adding a horizontal sashing strip between each row. Sew a horizontal sashing strip to the top and bottom of the quilt center. Refer to the diagram on page 47, if necessary.

6 border

Cut (8) 7" strips across the width of the border fabric. Sew the strips together end-to-end to make 1 long strip. Trim the borders from this strip.

Refer to Borders (pg. 102) in the Construction Basics to measure and cut the borders. The strips are approximately 80" for the sides and approximately 77½" for the top and bottom.

7 quilt & bind

Layer the quilt with batting and backing and quilt. After the quilting is complete, square up the quilt and trim away all excess batting and backing. Add binding to complete the quilt. See Construction Basics (pg. 102) for binding instructions.

4A

1 Sew a 1½" black strip to the top of a 4" white strip.

2 Cut the strip set into 5" segments.

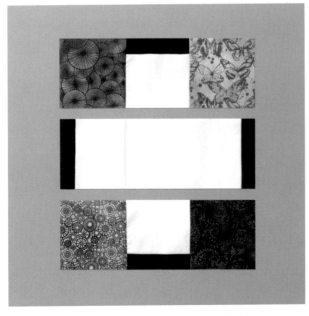

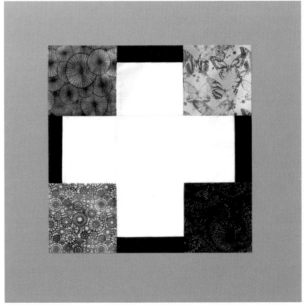

3 Select 4 print squares, (4) 5" segments, and 1 white square. Arrange the pieces in 3 rows of 3 as shown and sew together into rows.

4 Sew the rows together to complete the block. Make 20.

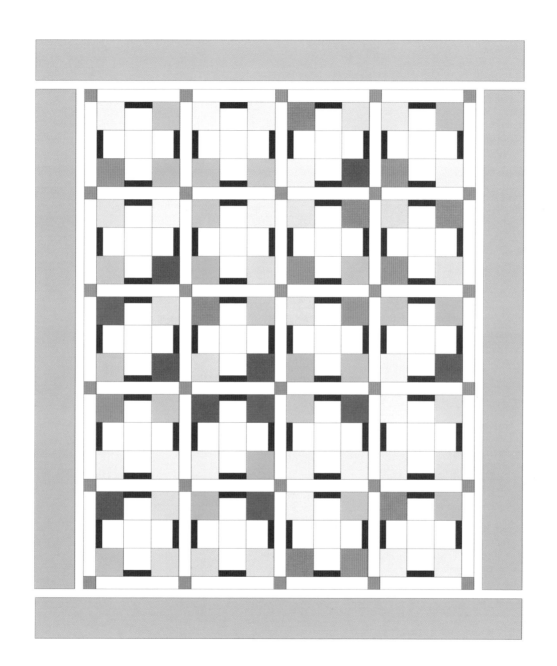

For the tutorial and everything you need to make this quilt visit: www.msqc.co/blokfall19

tile style

As Veterans Day draws near, my thoughts turn to the countless men and women who have served in our armed forces. Dorthea (Dot) Daley Engel was one of those brave heroes, and she grew up right here in our sleepy little town of Hamilton, Missouri.

As a young nurse, Dot joined the army and was sent to serve at a military hospital in the Philippines. Pearl Harbor was attacked, and the next day the Japanese military bombed the hospital where Dot was stationed. Dot and her fellow nurses sprang to action, dragging their patients to the safety of the surrounding wilderness. In the jungles of Bataan, she faced unimaginable dangers, yet was able to set aside her fear and discomfort to tend to those in her care. She spoke of her experience in an interview for *The American Magazine* in October 1942:

"Little did I dream that I would soon be trying to care for patients on beds set in the middle of a sandy river bed, that snakes would hang down from the bamboo and mango trees which sheltered us from Japanese bombing, that monkeys would chatter through the trees and try to steal what little food we had, that we would bathe in a creek. That we would always be hungry, always frightened. That we would grab shovels and help dig fox holes so we would have some shelter to crawl into when the dive bombers came. That we would all suffer from malaria and dysentery and diarrhea. It was a good thing for all of us that we had no idea what we were getting into."

In the midst of those trying conditions, something wholly unexpected took place: Dot fell in love. She and Lt. Emanuel Engel, known to his friends as "Boots," were married in a foxhole during a bombing.

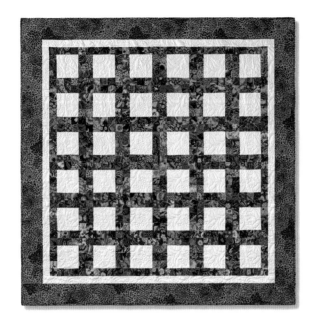

Tragically, Boots was captured and lost during the Bataan Death March. Though he was never heard from again, Dot held onto the hope that he had somehow survived.

After months of misery in Bataan, Dot narrowly escaped becoming a prisoner herself. She and some of her colleagues were evacuated to Australia to prepare to return to the U.S. Just one month later, on May 6, 1942, all 54 of the nurses remaining in Bataan were taken as prisoners of war. They were not liberated until February 3, 1945.

Back at home in Hamilton, Missouri, Dot continued waiting for any word on her husband's whereabouts. She refused widow's pay from the Army and did everything in her power to find him, but he was never found. It was a love story cut short, one with no fairytale ending. Dot lived out the remainder of her life just as sweet and ordinary as any other small-town nurse. She worked with her brother, Dr. Frank Daley, and faithfully served her patients for years.

Dot's is a story that should be told from generation to generation. When we speak of her goodness and selflessness, it kindles a deep appreciation for the sacrifices that have been made by countless veterans, but not only that, it instills in our hearts the desire to be a little kinder, to give more service, to extend greater compassion, to be better people.

Dot passed from this life on July 2, 2004, at the age of 88. She was an example of the best humanity has to offer, and we are so proud to call her one of our very own hometown heroes.

materials

QUILT SIZE
75" x 75"

BLOCK SIZE
10" finished

QUILT TOP
1 roll 2½" print strips
1¾ yards background fabric
   - includes inner border

OUTER BORDER
1½ yards

BINDING
¾ yard

BACKING
4¾ yards - vertical seam(s)

SAMPLE QUILT
Kaffe Fassett Collective Stash Blue Florals by Kaffe Fasset for FreeSpirit Fabrics

1 cut

From the background fabric, cut (6) 6½" strips across the width of the fabric. Subcut (6) 6½" squares from each strip for a **total of 36** background squares. Set the remaining fabric aside for now.

2 make strip sets

Select (15) 2½" print strips. Sew (3) 2½" print strips together lengthwise, using a ¼" seam allowance. **Make 5** strip sets.

Press. Cut each strip set into (16) 2½" increments to make 3-patch units. Repeat for a **total of (72)** 3-patch units. **2A**

Using the remaining (25) 2½" print strips, sew (5) 2½" print strips together lengthwise, using a ¼" seam allowance. **Make 5** strip sets.

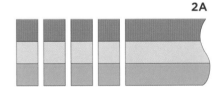

2A

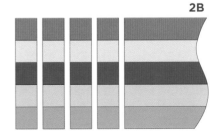

2B

Press. Cut each strip set into (16) 2½" increments to make 5-patch units. Repeat for a **total of (72)** 5-patch units. **2B**

3 block construction

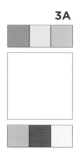

3A

Sew 2 differing 3-patch units to the top and bottom of a 6½" square. Open and press the seams toward the square. **3A**

Sew 2 differing 5-patch units to either side of the square. Open and press the seams toward the square. **3B**

Make 36 blocks. **3C**

Block Size: 10" finished

4 arrange & sew

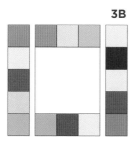

3B

Lay out your blocks in **6 rows** of **6 blocks** each. Sew blocks together in rows. Press the seam allowances of all odd rows to the left and all even rows to the right. Nest the seams and sew the rows together.

5 inner border

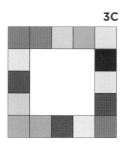

3C

Cut (7) 2½" strips across the width of the background fabric. Sew the strips end-to-end to make 1 long strip. Trim the inner borders from this strip.

Refer to Borders (pg. 102) in the Construction Basics to measure and cut the inner borders. Trim the inner borders from this strip. The strips are approximately 60½" for the sides and approximately 64½" for the top and bottom.

6 outer border

From the outer border fabric, cut (7) 6" strips across the width of the fabric. Sew the strips together end-to-end to make 1 long strip. Trim the outer borders from this strip.

Refer to Borders (pg. 102) in the Construction Basics to measure and cut the outer borders. The strips are approximately 64½" for the sides and approximately 75½" for the top and bottom.

7 quilt & bind

Layer the quilt with batting and backing and quilt. After the quilting is complete, square up the quilt and trim away all excess batting and backing. Add binding to complete the quilt. See Construction Basics (pg. 102) for binding instructions.

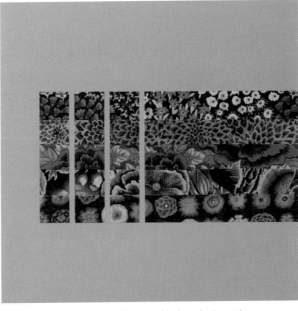

1 Sew (3) 2½" print strips together lengthwise, using a ¼" seam allowance. Make 5 strip sets. Press. Cut each strip set into (16) 2½" increments to make 3-patch units. You will need a total of (72) 3-patch units.

2 Sew (5) 2½" print strips together lengthwise, using a ¼" seam allowance. Make 5 strip sets. Cut each strip set into (16) 2½" increments to make 5-patch units. You will need a total of (72) 5-patch units.

3 Sew 2 differing 3-patch units to the top and bottom of a 6½" square.

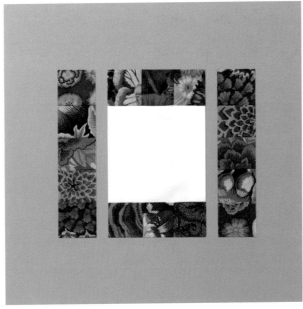

4 Sew 2 different 5-patch units to either side of the square.

5 Open and press the block.

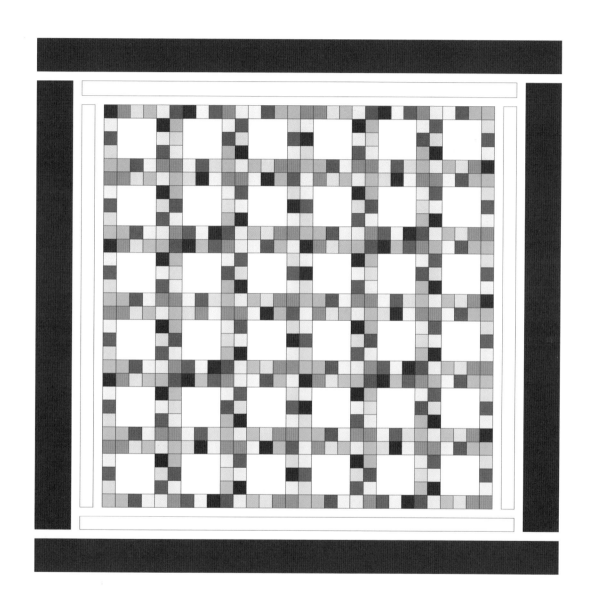

waves

"You see, it's very tedious being stuck up here all day long with a pole up your back!" That's what the lovable scarecrow from *The Wizard of Oz* says to Dorothy right before she frees him and they dance down the yellow brick road together. Come to think of it, who's idea was it to put a man made of straw on a pole and stick him in a field?

These straw-stuffed friends of ours have been the guardians of crop fields long before they took us to Emerald City and became a fall decor favorite! The scarecrow's story began in the golden wheat fields of Egypt, a favorite hangout spot for flocks of hungry quail. Egyptian farmers needed to find a way to keep quail from feeding on their seeds and wheat, so they placed tall wooden frames strung up with nets in the fields, inadvertently creating the very first scarecrow. Even though it didn't talk or sing, it still worked beautifully for the farmers because they were able to protect their crops and catch dinner all at once!

The ancient Greeks got a bit more creative with their scarecrows. Greek farmers would carve them in the likeness of Priapus, the son of the god Dionysus and goddess Aphrodite. According to Greek mythology, Priapus would ensure good harvests for

For the tutorial and everything you need to make this quilt visit:
www.msqc.co/blockfall19

farmers and vintners because he was supposedly so ugly birds scattered at the very sight of him. Poor Priapus! In Pilgrim communities, families would take turns guarding the crop fields themselves, chasing off any pesky birds that came near. As America began to expand west, scarecrows became popular amongst farmers and were typically made from wood and straw like the kind we're familiar with today. After World War II, some farmers began building scarecrows that whirled around like windmills to scare off hungry birds.

Even though farmers have developed more modern methods of protecting their crops, we still see scarecrows in fields today! They've become charming, smiling symbols for bountiful harvests, popular fall decorations, and fun quilting projects! Speaking of which, does your scrap stash steadily continue to grow? Well, a proper scarecrow requires clothes just like the rest of us, right? Instead of buying new fabric, you could put all those scraps to use by sewing a colorful shirt, pants, or overalls for a homemade scarecrow this season! You can find all sorts of patterns and tutorials on DIY scarecrows online, whether it's starting from scratch with a plank of wood or learning how to make a happy scarecrow face with some leftover batting and burlap. Feeling inspired now that you know a bit more about scarecrows? Take that inspiration to your scrap pile so you can have a charming scarecrow friend just like Dorothy!

materials

QUILT SIZE
86" x 103½"

BLOCK SIZE
17½" finished

QUILT TOP
1 package 10" print squares
1 package 10" background squares

INNER BORDER
¾ yard

OUTER BORDER
1¾ yards

BINDING
¾ yard

BACKING
9¼ yards - vertical seam(s)
   or 3¼ yards of 108" wide

OTHER
Missouri Star Drunkard's Path Large
   Circle Template Set

SAMPLE QUILT
Liberty Star by Kim Diehl for Henry
Glass Fabrics

1 layer & cut

Set 2 background squares and 2 print squares aside for another project.

Layer a background square with a print square. Place template B on a corner of the layered squares, align the 2 sides of the template with the fabric, and cut along the curve. Align the 9½" mark of template A on the opposite corner of the layered squares. Cut around the 2 sides of the template and the curve.

Repeat with 19 additional print squares and 19 additional background squares. You will have a **total of 20** each of the

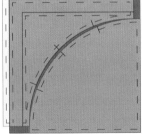

1A

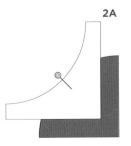

2A

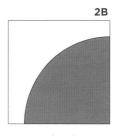

2B

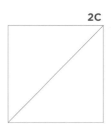

2C

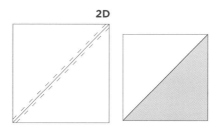

2D

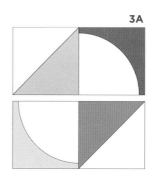

3A

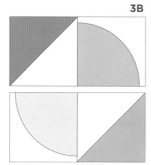

3B

A and B pieces cut from prints and a **total of 20** each of the A and B pieces cut from the background. **1A**

2 sew

Make Drunkard's Path Units

Pair all print A pieces with background B pieces and all background A pieces with print B pieces.

Pick up an A/B set. Fold each piece in half on the diagonal and finger press to mark the midway point of each curved edge. Alternatively, you can also use the registration marks on the templates to mark 3 points along both curves of each piece. Pin at the center point and both ends of the seam allowance. If you marked additional points from the template pin at those points as well. **2A**

Stitch the 2 pieces together along the curve. Use your fingers to ease in the fullness around the curve and avoid stretching the fabric as you sew. Press the seam allowance towards the A piece. Measure 9¼" from the corner of the B piece horizontally and trim the unit. Measure 9¼" from the corner of the B piece vertically and trim the unit. Make a **total of 40** drunkard's path units. **2B**

Make Half-Square Triangles

Mark a diagonal line on the reverse side of the remaining background squares. **2C**

Place the background square right sides together with a print square. Sew on either side of the marked line with a ¼" seam allowance. Cut on the marked line.

Open and press to reveal 2 half-square triangles. Trim each half-square triangle to 9¼". **Make 40** half-square triangles. **2D**

3 block construction

Select 2 half-square triangle units and 2 drunkard's path units with print A pieces. Arrange the 4 units in 2 rows of 2 as shown. Sew together in rows. Press the seam of the top row to the right and the seam of the bottom row to the left. Nest the seams and sew the rows together to complete the A block. **3A**

Make 10 A blocks.

Block Size: 17½" finished

Select 2 half-square triangle units and 2 drunkard's path units with background A pieces. Arrange the 4 units in 2 rows of 2 as shown. Sew together in rows. Press the seam of the top row to the right and the seam of the bottom row to the left. Nest the seams and sew the rows together to complete the B block. **3B**

Make 10 B blocks.

Block Size: 17½" finished

4 arrange & sew

Refer to the diagram on page 63 and lay out the blocks in rows, paying particular attention to how each block is oriented and the A and B blocks are alternated. Each row is made up of **4 blocks** and **5 rows** are needed. After the blocks have been sewn into rows, press the seam allowances of the odd rows toward the right and the even rows toward the left to make the seams nest.

Sew the rows together to complete the center of the quilt.

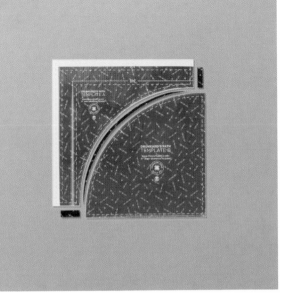

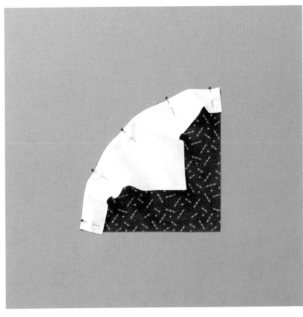

1 Place template B on a corner of the 10" squares and cut along the curve. Align the 9½" mark on template A with the remaining corner of the 10" square. Cut around the curve and the 2 sides of the template.

2 Mark the center of the arc on a background A piece and a print B piece. Line up the center marks and pin. Pin at both ends and any additional points you wish along the curve.

3 Sew along the curve removing the pins as you come to them. Press toward the A piece. Make 20. Repeat and make 20 drunkard's path units using print A pieces and background B pieces.

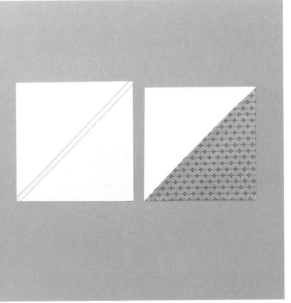

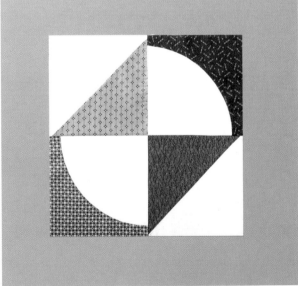

4 Mark a diagonal line on the reverse side of a background square. Place the marked square right sides together with a print square. Sew on both sides of the marked line. Cut on the marked line and open to reveal 2 half-square triangles. Make 40.

5 Select 2 drunkard's path units with the print A piece and 2 half-square triangles units. Lay out in a 4-patch formation as shown and sew together to complete Block A. Make 10.

6 Select 2 drunkard's path units with the background A piece and 2 half-square triangles units. Lay out in a 4-patch formation as shown and sew together to complete Block B. Make 10.

5 inner borders

From the inner border fabric, cut (9) 2½" strips across the width of the fabric. Sew the strips together end-to-end to make 1 long strip. Trim the border from this strip.

Refer to Borders (pg. 102) in the Construction Basics to measure and cut the inner borders. The strips are approximately 88" for the sides and 74½" for the top and bottom.

6 outer borders

From the outer border fabric, cut (9) 6½" strips across the width of the fabric. Sew the strips together end-to-end to make 1 long strip. Trim the borders from this strip.

Refer to Borders (pg. 102) in the Construction Basics to measure and cut the outer borders. The strips are approximately 92" for the sides and 86½" for the top and bottom.

7 quilt & bind

Layer the quilt with batting and backing and quilt. After the quilting is complete, square up the quilt and trim away all excess batting and backing. Add binding to complete the quilt. See Construction Basics (pg. 102) for binding instructions.

For the tutorial and everything you need to make this quilt visit:
www.msqc.co/blockfall19

sunshine
lattice

Fall is an introspective time for me; it's perfect for slowing down and taking the time to think, plan, and dream while the leaves are fluttering past my window. It's a time when I love getting out my journal after a busy day, settling down in a comfy chair, and writing out my thoughts. I am a journaler and while I don't write every day, I do write several times a week. My journal has become a comfort, a friend, and a record of my life. When I was younger, I didn't always write consistently, but I have now for many years. Journaling keeps me aware of the things that matter most.

In this overwhelmingly digital age, many people are longing to return to things that make them feel grounded, and what could be less digital than opening up a blank journal page and writing in it with an actual pencil? What a concept! Journaling is healing—it helps us sort through emotions and remember what's most important. It can even boost our mood and improve our memory. If you're having trouble sleeping, try writing out your thoughts before your head hits the pillow. It just might do the trick!

Journaling has become so much more than a record of our thoughts, now it's an art form, combining detailed drawings with to-do lists, charts, calendars, moods, thoughts, inspiration, and much, much more. I am amazed at people who are able to track their lives in such a wonderful way! I also enjoy drawing in my journals. It's where I work out some of my quilting ideas. And while I don't necessarily have an art journal, I do occasionally draw out a border, a quilt block, or a pretty flower. It's where I write out my grocery lists, things to remember, notes on a good talk I heard in church, quotes I like, and if I happen to be sitting by a grandchild, a tracing of their little hand.

Quilt journaling is a natural extension of the popular visual journals that so many are creating nowadays, but what if a completely blank page seems daunting? I don't always have the time to sketch out every little detail, add a cute border, and color in a quilt design. But, if a template existed, well, that would be right up my alley! I thought I'd give you all a leg up with this idea and include a simple template to help you track your projects right here.

QUILT PLANNER

PROJECT

SIZE _____ X _____

FABRICS _____

COLORS

PRECUTS

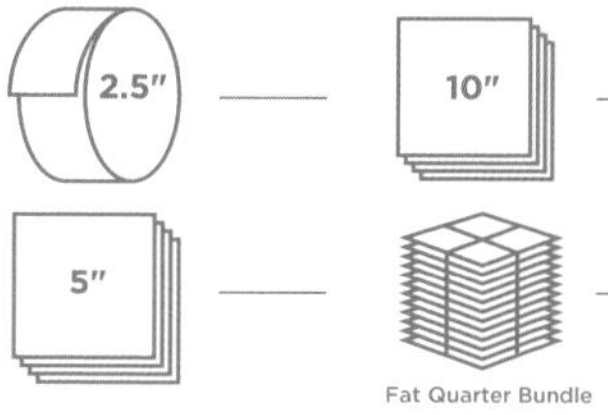

2.5" _____

10" _____

5" _____

Fat Quarter Bundle

BLOCK DESIGN

SIZE _____ X _____

BLOCKS _____

NOTES _____

SKETCH

Print off copies of this Quilt Planner and use for all your quilting projects

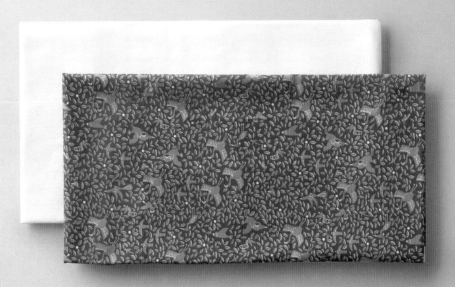
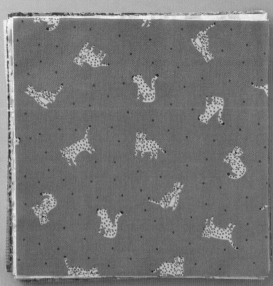

materials

QUILT SIZE
88" x 96"

BLOCK SIZE
18" x 8" finished

QUILT TOP
1 package 10" print squares
1 package 10" background squares
1½ yards background fabric
-includes inner border

OUTER BORDER
¼ yard

OUTER BORDER
1¾ yards

BINDING
¾ yard

BACKING
8¾ yards - vertical seam(s)
or 3 yards of 108" wide

SAMPLE QUILT
Under the Canopy by Citrus and Mint
Designs for Riley Blake Designs

1 cut

Set (2) 10" print squares aside for another project. Cut each of the remaining 10" print squares in half once to yield (2) 5" x 10" rectangles. A **total of 80** print rectangles are needed.

Set (2) 10" background squares aside for another project. Cut each of the remaining 10" background squares in half once to yield (2) 5" x 10" rectangles. A **total of 80** background rectangles are needed.

From the 1½ yards of background fabric, cut (18) 2½" strips across the width of the fabric. Set 8 strips aside for the inner border. Subcut the 10 remaining strips

into 2½" squares. Each strip will yield 16 squares and a **total of 160** are needed.

2 sew

On the reverse side of (40) 5" x 10" background rectangles, draw a line from corner to corner once on the diagonal with the line going from the lower right corner to the upper left corner. On the reverse side of the remaining (40) 5" x 10" background rectangles, draw a line from corner to corner once on the diagonal with the line going from the lower left corner to the upper right corner. **2A**

Place a marked background rectangle atop a print rectangle as shown with

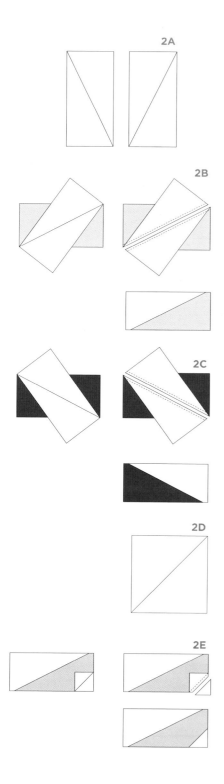

2A

2B

2C

2D

2E

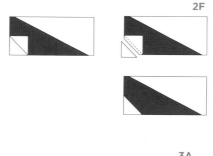

2F

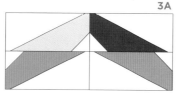

3A

right sides facing. Notice that the marked line is running from the lower left to the upper right. Sew on both sides of the drawn line using a ¼" seam allowance. Cut along the drawn line, open each to reveal 2 units. Press the seam allowance toward the darker fabric. You will have a **total of 80** units. We'll call these A units for clarity. **2B**

Place a marked background rectangle atop a print rectangle as shown with right sides facing. Notice that the marked line is running from the lower right to the upper left. Sew on both sides of the drawn line using a ¼" seam allowance. Cut along the drawn line, open each to reveal 2 units. Press the seam allowance toward the darker fabric. You will have a **total of 80** units. We'll call these B units for clarity. **2C**

Trim all A and B units to 9½" x 4½".

Mark a diagonal line on the reverse side of each of the 2½" background squares. **2D**

Place a marked background square on top of an A unit with right sides facing. Sew on the marked line. Trim the excess fabric ¼" away from the sewn seam. Press. **2E**

Repeat to make a **total of 80** A units.

Place a marked background square on top of a B unit with right sides facing. Sew on the marked line. Trim the excess fabric ¼" away from the sewn seam. Press. **2F**

Repeat to make a **total of 80** B units.

3 block construction

Arrange 2 A units and 2 B units into a 4-patch formation as shown. Sew the top 2 units together and press the seam to the right. Sew the bottom 2 units together and press the seam to the left. Nest the seams and sew the 2 rows together to complete the block. **3A**

Make 40 blocks.

Block Size: 18" x 8"

4 arrange & sew

Lay out the blocks in rows, making note of the orientation of the blocks in the diagram on page 71. Each row is made up of **4 blocks** and **10 rows** are needed. After the blocks have been sewn into rows, press the seam allowances of the odd rows toward the right and the even rows toward the left to make the seams nest.

Sew the rows together to complete the center of the quilt.

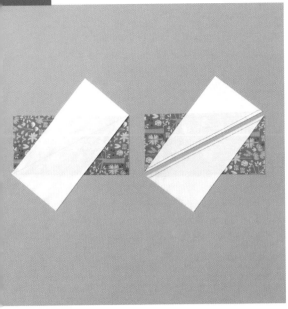

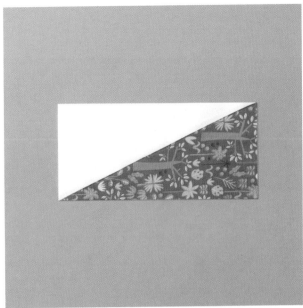

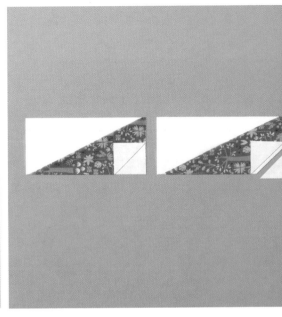

1 Draw a diagonal line on the reverse side of a background rectangle. Lay the marked rectangle on top of a print rectangle with right sides facing as shown. Sew on either side of the marked line with a ¼" seam allowance and cut on the marked line.

2 Open to reveal 2 half-rectangle triangles and press toward the dark side.

3 Mark a diagonal line on the reverse side of a background square. Lay the marked square on top of the print corner of a half-rectangle triangle, right sides facing. Sew on the marked line and cut away the excess fabric.

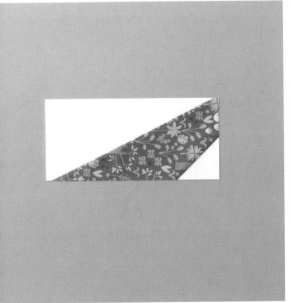

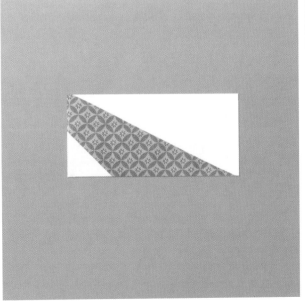

4 Press toward the dark fabric to complete the A unit. Make 80.

5 Mark a diagonal line on the reverse side of a background rectangle oriented opposite of the lines you marked previously. Follow the previous steps to create a B unit, which is a mirror of the A units. Make 80.

6 Arrange 2 A units and 2 B units into a 4-patch formation as shown. Sew together in pairs. Then sew the pairs together to complete the block. Make 40.

5 inner border

Pick up the (8) 2½" strips you set aside earlier. Sew the strips together end-to-end to make 1 long strip. Trim the border from this strip.

Refer to Borders (pg. 102) in the Construction Basics to measure and cut the inner borders. The strips are approximately 80½" for the sides and 76½" for the top and bottom.

6 outer border

From the outer border fabric, cut (9) 6½" strips across the width of the fabric. Sew the strips together end-to-end to make 1 long strip. Trim the borders from this strip.

Refer to Borders (pg. 102) in the Construction Basics to measure and cut the outer borders. The strips are approximately 84½" for the sides and 88½" for the top and bottom.

7 quilt & bind

Layer the quilt with batting and backing and quilt. After the quilting is complete, square up the quilt and trim away all excess batting and backing. Add binding to complete the quilt. See Construction Basics (pg. 102) for binding instructions.

half-square triangle hooks

On my travels to visit quilters across the U.S., I often find myself in the most interesting little towns. I love to get a sense of the history of a place I'm visiting and one of the best ways to do this isn't always going to a museum. Instead, I like to go to local antique shops and thrift stores. For years, I've collected all kinds of neat little items related to sewing, from old-fashioned irons to vintage sewing machines. Imagining how they were used makes me feel very grateful for the wonderfully efficient, easy-to-use sewing machines we have today.

It was only a little more than 250 years ago when a man named Charles Fredrick Weisenthal invented an ingenious device to help make hand sewing easier. It had a double-pointed needle with an eye at one end. After him, there was a succession of inventors who also continued to refine this idea, eventually leading up to the modern sewing machine.

Thomas Saint, an English inventor, is the one who technically invented the first sewing machine prototype, but he never profited from his invention. It was meant to be used for working with leather. He titled the patent for his clever machine: "An Entire New Method of Making and Completing Shoes, Boots, Spatterdashes, Clogs, and Other Articles, by Means of Tools and Machines also Invented by Me for that Purpose, and of Certain Compositions of the Nature of Japan or Varnish, which will be

For the tutorial and everything you need to make this quilt visit:
www.msqc.co/blockfall19

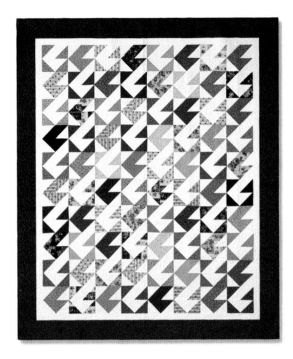

very advantageous in many useful Appliances." What a mouthful! But most importantly, he invented a way to mechanically chain stitch.

At the beginning of the 1800s, an Austrian tailor named Josef Madersperger improved upon earlier designs and developed a machine that initially sewed only in straight lines using Saint's chain stitch, but was eventually capable of stitching small circles and ovals as well as embroidered designs. Sadly, he never sold his machine either and died penniless.

Soon, a more practical sewing machine would be invented, by Barthélemy Thimonnier, a French tailor. His machine also used Saint's chain stitch. In 1830, he began a company to create uniforms for the French Army using his sewing machine, but his success was short-lived. His factory burned down and that was the end of that.

After many more attempts at refining the sewing machine, widespread commercial success was finally achieved by a man named Isaac Merritt Singer in 1851. The Singer name is now synonymous with sewing machines, and for a good reason. Being an engineer, when Singer first glimpsed a sewing machine, he saw a lot of room for improvement! His new machine mounted the needle vertically, included a presser foot to keep fabric from shifting, had a fixed arm, a basic tension system, and a foot pedal. Can you imagine a sewing machine any other way?

Thank goodness for all the efforts that have gone into creating sewing machines. Without them, I don't think I would be doing much quilting!

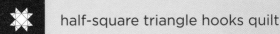

materials

QUILT SIZE
79" x 95"

BLOCK SIZE
8" finished

QUILT TOP
1 package 10" print squares
1 package 10" background squares

INNER BORDER
¾ yard

OUTER BORDER
1¾ yards

BINDING
¾ yard

BACKING
5¾ yards - vertical seam(s)
    or 3 yards of 108" wide

OTHER
Clearly Perfect Slotted Trimmer A

SAMPLE QUILT
Hat Box by Andover Fabrics

1 sew

Select 2 print squares and 2 background squares to set aside for another project. Draw a line from corner to corner twice on the diagonal on the reverse side of each remaining background square. Layer a marked background square with a print square with right sides facing. Sew on both sides of each line using a ¼" seam allowance. Cut each set of sewn squares in half vertically and horizontally, then cut on the drawn lines. Use the Clearly Perfect Slotted Trimmer A to square each half-square triangle unit to 4½" and trim off the dog ears. Open and press the seam allowance toward the darker fabric. Each set of sewn squares will yield 8 half-square triangles and a **total of 320** are needed for the quilt. **1A**

Note: When cutting the half-square triangles, place 4 of the matching half-square triangle units into a pile for making the A blocks and the other 4 matching half-square triangle units into a second pile for making the B blocks. Doing this now will ensure that you distribute the fabrics evenly between the A and B blocks.

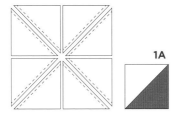

1A

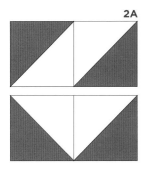

2A

2B

2 block construction

Block A

Using the stack of half-square triangle units for the A blocks, pick up 4 matching half-square triangle units and arrange them in a 4-patch formation as shown. Sew the half-square triangle units together in rows. Press the seam of the top row to the right and the seam of the bottom row to the left. Nest the seams and sew the rows together to complete the block. **2A**

Make 40.

Block Size: 8″ finished

Block B

Using the stack of half-square triangle units for the B blocks, pick up 4 matching half-square triangle units and arrange them in a 4-patch formation as shown. Sew the half-square triangle units together in rows. Press the seam of the top row to the right and the seam of the bottom row to the left. Nest the seams and sew the rows together to complete the block. **2B**

Make 40.

Block Size: 8″ finished

3 arrange & sew

Refer to the diagram on page 79 and lay out the blocks in rows, paying particular attention to how the A and B blocks are alternated. Each row is made up of **8 blocks** and **10 rows** are needed. After the blocks have been sewn into rows, press the seam allowances of the odd-numbered rows toward the right and the even-numbered rows to the left to make the seams nest.

Sew the rows together to complete the center of the quilt.

4 inner border

Cut (8) 2½″ strips across the width of the fabric. Sew the strips together end-to-end to make 1 long strip. Trim the borders from this strip.

Refer to Borders (pg. 102) in the Construction Basics to measure and cut the inner borders. The strips are approximately 80½″ for the sides and approximately 68½″ for the top and bottom.

5 outer border

Cut (9) 6″ strips across the width of the fabric. Sew the strips together end-to-end to make 1 long strip. Trim the borders from this strip.

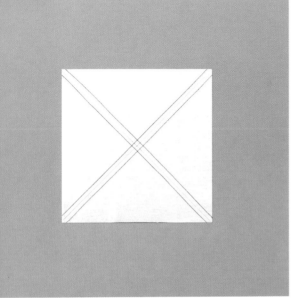

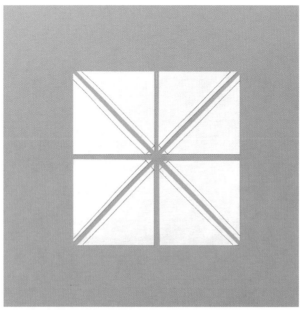

1 Mark a line corner to corner on both diagonal on the reverse side of a background square. Sew on both sides of the marked lines using a ¼" seam allowance.

2 Cut the sewn squares in half vertically and horizontally, then on the drawn lines. Trim each unit to 4½". Open each unit and press toward the darker fabric.

3 Pick up 4 matching half-square triangle units and arrange them in a 4-patch formation as shown. Sew together to form rows. Press the seam in the top row to the right and the bottom row to the left.

4 Nest the seams and sew the rows together to complete a Block A.

5 Pick up the 4 remaining matching half-square triangle units and arrange them in a 4-patch formation as shown. Sew together to form rows. Press the seam in the top row to the right and the bottom row to the left.

6 Nest the seams and sew the rows together to complete the Block B.

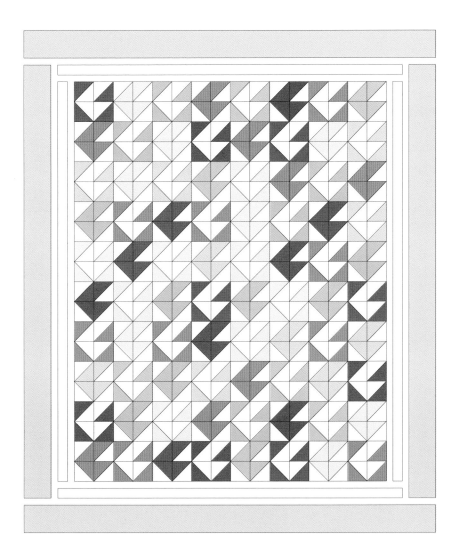

Refer to Borders (pg. 102) in the Construction Basics to measure and cut the outer borders. The strips are approximately 84½″ for the sides and approximately 79½″ for the top and bottom.

6 quilt & bind

Layer the quilt with batting and backing and quilt. After the quilting is complete, square up the quilt and trim away all excess batting and backing. Add binding to complete the quilt. See Construction Basics (pg. 102) for binding instructions.

bud bouquet

Have you ever heard the old superstition about black cats? Some believe that if they cross your path, you're in for a bout of bad luck. I'm a cat lover and anytime a cat crosses my path I consider myself lucky! All furry little creatures should be treated well and, unfortunately, many black cats and black dogs have difficulty being adopted. Perhaps it's due to age-old stereotypes, silly superstitions, or even being perceived as more aggressive, but it breaks my heart. The good news is, awareness is spreading due to events like National Black Dog Day on October 1st and Black Cat Appreciation Day on August 17th. My friend, Jamie, adopted a wonderful black dog and this is her story.

"One Saturday morning, we woke up early and went to look at dogs at a shelter near our home called 'Family Dog's New Life Shelter.' They often brought dogs in from neighboring states to save them from being put down. There were many people lined up in the waiting room to see all the new dogs, but I had looked at the website the night before and was drawn to a certain one. His name was Kola, he was a chow mix, and his description said that he was friendly. I wasn't sure what would happen, but I was hoping we would get to meet him.

"Before our turn came up, Kola was taken into a private room to meet another family. I was nervous because I had a feeling that he might be the right dog for us. Thankfully, they passed him up and moved on to another dog. We requested to see him first and as soon as we met him, he hopped up on the couch next to us and

For the tutorial and everything you need to make this quilt visit:
www.msqc.co/blockfall19

licked our faces. He was the furriest black dog I'd ever met, but he had beautiful golden eyes and a happy demeanor, even though he looked pretty wild. His coat hadn't been groomed for quite awhile and it practically touched the floor, but his personality won us over. We couldn't say no to such a sweet dog.

"When we adopted Kola, we were given his story along with his paperwork. He came from a family that left him behind in their backyard when they moved away. He quickly escaped and went looking for food and shelter around his neighborhood. He found a kind neighbor who

took him in for a while but soon he was at another shelter where he lived for almost a year without being adopted. Finally, he took the long trip up to our state where we met him.

"We immediately gave Kola a bath and a haircut, and boy did he need it! It took some time to scrub him clean, but he enjoyed every minute of it. As we lathered up his neck, he closed his eyes and relaxed. Next came the clippers. All the overgrown fur fell away to reveal a very handsome black dog with white markings on his chest and chin. He was absolutely transformed. With the weight of all that fur gone, he hopped all over the yard, rolling in the grass. At the beginning of his new life, we decided he needed a new name. We called him 'Kuma,' which means 'bear' in Japanese. This little black bear has been a gentle companion to us for more than five years now and we can't imagine life without him."

materials

QUILT SIZE
63¼" x 63¼"

BLOCK SIZE
12" finished

QUILT TOP
2 packages 5" print squares
¾ yard background fabric –
   includes border

SETTING TRIANGLES
2 yards

BINDING
¾ yard

BACKING
4 yards - vertical seam(s)

SAMPLE QUILT
Royal Blue by Edyta Sitar for Andover Fabrics

1 sort & cut

Sort the packages of 5" squares into lights and darks. The stack of light squares must contain 36 squares. The stack of dark squares must contain 45 squares. Set all remaining squares aside.

Select 9 squares from the light stack and trim them to 4½".

Select 18 squares from the dark stack and trim them to 4½".

2 sew

On the reverse side of the remaining 27 light squares, draw a line from corner to corner once on the diagonal. **2A**

2A

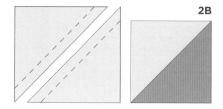

2B

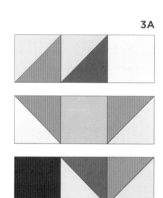

3A

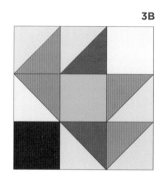

3B

Lay each marked light square atop a dark square, right sides facing. Sew on either side of the marked line using a ¼" seam allowance. Cut each set of sewn squares on the marked line. Open and press the seam allowance toward the darker fabric. Each set of sewn squares will yield 2 half-square triangles and a **total of 54** are needed for the quilt. Trim each half-square triangle unit to 4½". **2B**

3 construct blocks

Select 6 half-square triangle units, (1) 4½" light square, and (2) 4½" dark squares. Lay them out in 3 rows of 3 as shown. Sew the pieces together in rows. Press the seam allowances in the top and bottom rows to the right. Press the seam allowance in the middle row to the left. **3A**

Nest the seams and sew the rows together to complete the block.
Make 9. 3B

Block Size: 12" finished

4 make horizontal sashing strips

From the background fabric, cut (9) 2½" strips across the width of the fabric. Subcut 4 strips into 2½" x 12½" rectangles. Each strip will yield 3 rectangles and a **total of 12** are needed. Set the remaining 5 strips aside for the border.

From the setting triangle fabric, cut (1) 2½" strip across the width of the fabric and set the rest of the fabric aside for now. Subcut (4) 2½" squares from the strip and set the remainder of the strip aside for another project.

Sew a 2½" x 12½" rectangle to either side of a 2½" print square. Add a 2½" print square and end the row with another 2½" x 12½" rectangle. Press the seams toward the print squares. **Make 2. 4A**

5 arrange & sew

Note: The diagram on page 87 showing the assembly of this quilt shows the quilt center set on point. The side referred to as the "top of the quilt center" is the side shown in the top left corner of the diagram.

Lay out the blocks in **3 rows** with each row being made up of **3 blocks**. As you make each row, sew a 2½" x 12½" sashing rectangle between each block. Press the seam allowances of the sashing strips toward the sashing rectangles.

Sew the rows together adding a horizontal sashing strip between each row. Refer to the diagram on page 87, if necessary.

6 border

Pick up the (5) 2½" strips you set aside earlier. Sew the strips together end-to-end to make 1 long strip. Trim the borders from the strip.

4A

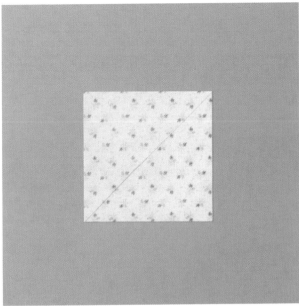

1 Draw a diagonal line on the reverse side of 27 light squares.

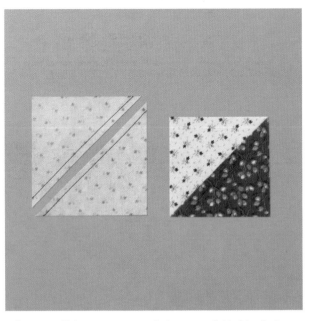

2 Lay a light square atop a dark square, right sides facing. Sew on both sides of the marked line using a ¼" seam allowance. Cut each set of sewn squares on the marked line. Open to reveal 2 half-square triangle units.

3 Select 6 half-square triangle units, (1) 4½" light square, and (2) 4½" dark squares. Arrange them in 3 rows of 3 as shown. Sew the pieces together in rows. Press the seams in the top and bottom rows to the right and the seams in the middle row to the left.

4 Nest the seams and sew the rows together to complete the block. Make 9.

Refer to Borders (pg. 102) in the Construction Basics to measure and cut the borders. The strips are approximately 40½″ for the sides and approximately 44½″ for the top and bottom.

7 setting triangles

From the setting triangle fabric, cut (2) 33″ strips across the width of the fabric. Subcut the strips into 33″ squares. Subcut each square once on the diagonal to yield a **total of 4** setting triangles.

Find and mark the center of the longest edge of each setting triangle. Find and mark the center of each outer edge of the quilt center. Line up the center of 1 setting triangle with the center of 1 side of the quilt center, right sides together. Pin in place. Sew the triangle to the quilt center with a ¼″ seam allowance. Press. Repeat to sew a setting triangle to the opposite side of the quilt center. Trim the ends of the setting triangles even with the edges of the quilt center.

Sew the 2 remaining setting triangles to the 2 remaining sides of the quilt center. Press the seams to complete the quilt top.

8 quilt & bind

Layer the quilt with batting and backing and quilt. After the quilting is complete, square up the quilt and trim away all excess batting and backing. Add binding to complete the quilt. See Construction Basics (pg. 102) for binding instructions.

tutorial reboot

original layout

They say you shouldn't cut corners, but with this beautiful Cornered Drunkard's Path block, that's exactly what you should do! Taking this traditional quilt block and adding cute little corners on it completely transforms it into a new, contemporary design. Although it may seem complicated with all those little pieces and curves, this pattern is as easy as can be, I promise!

Check out these variations on the original Cornered Drunkard's Path quilt. We've taken the online tutorial and given it a reboot here in Block just for you using the same steps, but with brand new results. It's amazing what a simple change in fabric or block orientation can do to make a pattern feel fresh. The first layout was a lot of fun to piece together and here are even more options for you to try out. What can you do with this clever pattern? I always love to see what a couple of flips and turns can do to a tried-and-true quilt block. Go ahead, stitch along with the original tutorial, play around with the blocks, and get inspired to make something absolutely beautiful and completely unique.

SUPPLY LIST

2¾ yards Solid Fabric

3 yards 24″ Wide Fusible

5 yards Background Fabric -
   includes Outer Border

Easy Circle Cut Ruler

4½ yards Backing

Option 1:

Make all of the units the same way described in the original pattern and tutorial. Change the orientation of the 4 units that make up each block as shown in the diagram above. Sew the blocks together in **7 rows** of **6 blocks** to create this quilt top.

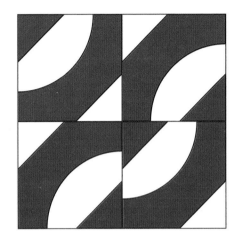

Option 2:

Reverse the colors on the original pattern to create this quilt top. The layout of this option is the same as the original, but the colors are reversed. Simply swap out the fabric requirements and placement of the colors to create this quilt top.

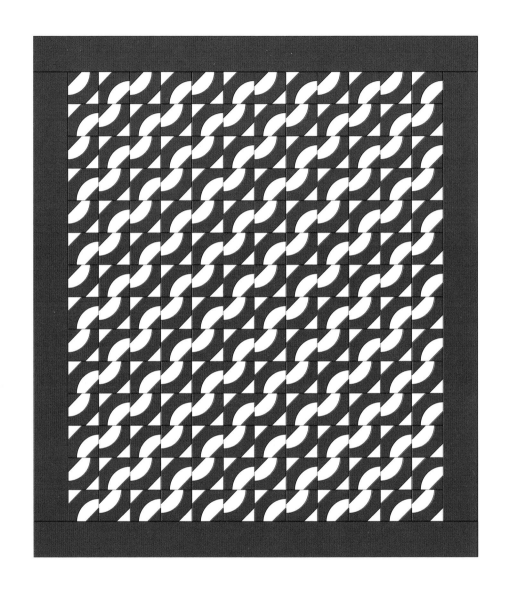

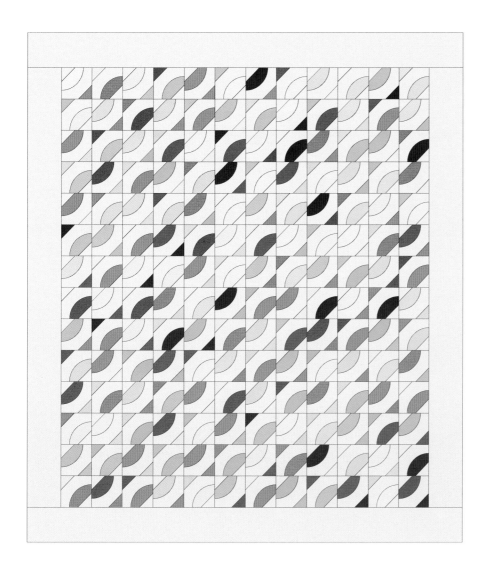

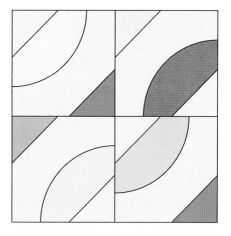

Option 3:

Make it scrappy! To substitute scraps for the red fabric used in the original, use (42) 7¾" squares and (168) 2½" squares in place of the solid fabric listed in the supply list. None of the other items on the supply list or instructions need to change to create this look.

bud
bouquet

QUILT SIZE
63¼" x 63¼"

BLOCK SIZE
12" finished

QUILT TOP
2 packages 5" print squares
¾ yard background fabric –
  includes border

SETTING TRIANGLES
2 yards

BINDING
¾ yard

BACKING
4 yards - vertical seam(s)

SAMPLE QUILT
Royal Blue by Edyta Sitar for
  Andover Fabrics

ONLINE TUTORIALS
msqc.co/blockfall19

QUILTING PATTERN
Bo Dangle

PATTERN
pg. 80

castle
wall

QUILT SIZE
72½" x 84½"

BLOCK SIZE
4½", 9½" x 4½", and
   14½" x 19½" finished

QUILT TOP
1 panel
1 package 10" print squares
¼ yard contrasting fabric

BORDER
1½ yards

BINDING
¾ yard

BACKING
5¼ yards - vertical seam(s)
   or 2¾ yards of 108" wide

SAMPLE QUILT
Bramble by Gingiber for Moda Fabrics

ONLINE TUTORIALS
msqc.co/blockfall19

QUILTING PATTERN
Flutterby

PATTERN
pg. 32

fancy
flight

QUILT SIZE
47" x 61"

BLOCK SIZE
4" x 2" finished

QUILT TOP
1 roll 2½" print strips*
¾ yard sashing fabric
   - includes inner border

OUTER BORDER
1 yard

BINDING
½ yard

BACKING
3¼ yards - horizontal seam(s)

*Strips need to be 42" of usable width. If your
fabric is less than 42" of usable width, add an
additional ¼ yard of a coordinating print fabric
and cut (2) 2½" strips and add them to your roll.

SAMPLE QUILT
Islander Batik by Kathy Engle for
Island Batik Fabrics

ONLINE TUTORIALS
msqc.co/blockfall19

QUILT PATTERN
Wind Swirls

PATTERN
pg. 14

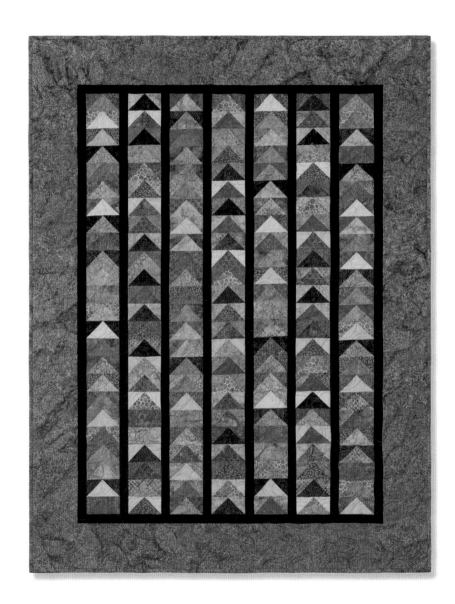

four square

QUILT SIZE
77" x 92½"

BLOCK SIZE
13½" finished

QUILT TOP
2 packages 5" print squares
½ yard black solid
2¾ yards white solid*
¼ yard coordinating print**

BORDER
1¾ yards

BINDING
¾ yard

BACKING
5¾ yards - vertical seams
    or 3 yards of 108" width

*The fabric you select needs to have a minimum
of 42" of usable width.
**Note: There is enough backing fabric included
that you can cut (2) 2½" strips from the
backing fabric to use for the coordinating print
if desired.

SAMPLE QUILT
Seasons by Jason Yenter for In
The Beginning Fabrics

ONLINE TUTORIALS
msqc.co/blockfall19

QUILT PATTERN
Sticky Buns

PATTERN
pg. 40

half-square triangle hooks

QUILT SIZE
79" x 95"

BLOCK SIZE
8" finished

QUILT TOP
1 package 10" print squares
1 package 10" background squares

INNER BORDER
¾ yard

OUTER BORDER
1¾ yards

BINDING
¾ yard

BACKING
5¾ yards - vertical seam(s)
    or 3 yards of 108" wide

OTHER
Clearly Perfect Slotted Trimmer A

SAMPLE QUILT
Hat Box by Andover Fabrics

ONLINE TUTORIALS
msqc.co/blockfall19

QUILT PATTERN
Meander

PATTERN
pg. 72

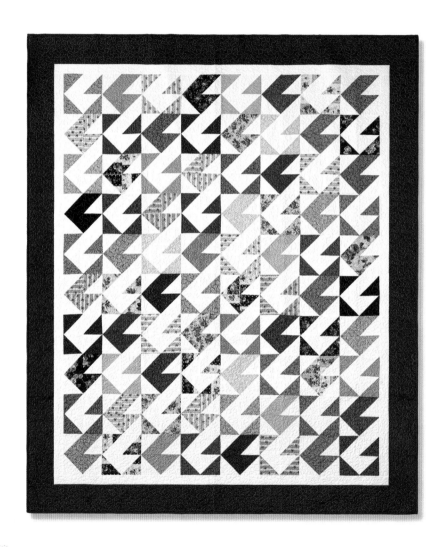

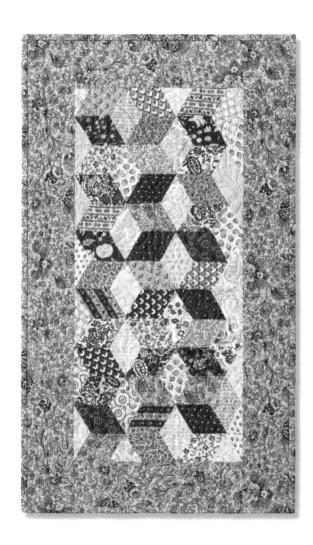

mini rhombus

TABLE RUNNER
33" x 18½"

PROJECT TOP
1 package 5" print squares

QUILT TOP
4 matching packages 5" print squares

BORDER
½ yard

BINDING
¼ yard

BACKING
¾ yard

OTHER
Missouri Star Mini Rhombus Template

SAMPLE QUILT
Chafarcani by French General
for Moda Fabrics

ONLINE TUTORIALS
msqc.co/blockfall19

QUILTING PATTERN
Botanical Blossoms

PATTERN
pg. 22

square knot

QUILT SIZE
72" x 72"

BLOCK SIZE
8" finished

QUILT TOP
1 roll 2½" print strips
1 roll 2½" background strips

INNER BORDER
¼ yard - matching the 2½"
    background strips

OUTER BORDER
1½ yards

BINDING
¾ yard

BACKING
4½ yards - vertical seam(s)

SAMPLE QUILT
Golden Days by Fancy Pants
Designs for Riley Blake

ONLINE TUTORIALS
msqc.co/blockfall19

QUILTING PATTERN
Paisley Feather

PATTERN
pg. 6

sunshine lattice

QUILT SIZE
88" x 96"

BLOCK SIZE
18" x 8" finished

QUILT TOP
1 package 10" print squares
1 package 10" background squares
1½ yards background fabric
  -includes inner border

OUTER BORDER
¼ yard

OUTER BORDER
1¾ yards

BINDING
¾ yard

BACKING
8¾ yards - vertical seam(s)
  or 3 yards of 108" wide

SAMPLE QUILT
Under the Canopy by Citrus and Mint
Designs for Riley Blake Designs

ONLINE TUTORIALS
msqc.co/blockfall19

QUILTING PATTERN
Fleur de Lis

PATTERN
pg. 64

tile
style

QUILT SIZE
75" x 75"

BLOCK SIZE
10" finished

QUILT TOP
1 roll 2½" print strips
1¾ yards background fabric
   - includes inner border

OUTER BORDER
1½ yards

BINDING
¾ yard

BACKING
4¾ yards - vertical seam(s)

SAMPLE QUILT
Kaffe Fassett Collective Stash
Blue Florals by Kaffe Fasset for
FreeSpirit Fabrics

ONLINE TUTORIALS
msqc.co/blockfall19

QUILTING PATTERN
Bo Dangle

PATTERN
pg. 48

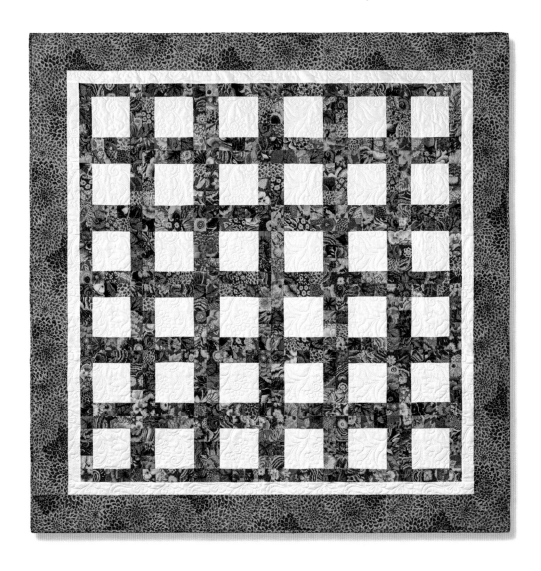

waves

QUILT SIZE
86" x 103½"

BLOCK SIZE
17½" finished

QUILT TOP
1 package 10" print squares
1 package 10" background squares

INNER BORDER
¾ yard

OUTER BORDER
1¾ yards

BINDING
¾ yard

BACKING
9¼ yards - vertical seam(s)
   or 3¼ yards of 108" wide

OTHER
Missouri Star Drunkard's Path Large
   Circle Template Set

SAMPLE QUILT
Liberty Star by Kim Diehl for Henry
Glass Fabrics

ONLINE TUTORIALS
msqc.co/blockfall19

QUILTING PATTERN
Free Swirls

PATTERN
pg. 56

construction basics

general quilting

- All seams are ¼" unless directions specify differently.
- Precuts are not prewashed; so do not prewash other fabrics in the project.
- Remove all selvages.

press seams

- Set the temperature of the iron on the cotton setting.
- Set the seam by pressing it just as it was sewn, right sides together.
- Place the darker fabric on top, lift, and press back.
- Press seam allowances toward the borders unless directed otherwise.

borders

- Always measure the quilt top in 3 different places vertically before cutting side borders.
- Start measuring about 4" in from the top and bottom.
- Take the average of those 3 measurements.
- Cut 2 border strips to that size. Piece strips together if needed.
- Attach one to either side of the quilt. Position the border fabric on top as you sew to prevent waviness and to keep the quilt straight.
- Repeat this process for the top and bottom borders, measuring the width 3 times. Include the newly attached side borders in your measurements.

backing

- Measure the quilt top vertically and horizontally. Add 8" to both measurements to make sure you have an extra 4" all the way around to make allowance for the fabric that is taken up in the quilting process as well as having adequate fabric for the quilting frame.
- Trim off all selvages and use a ½" seam allowance when piecing the backing. Sew the pieces together along the longest edge. Press the seam allowance open to decrease bulk.
- Use horizontal seams for smaller quilts (under 60" wide), vertical seams for larger quilts.
- Don't hesitate to cut a length of fabric in half along the fold line if it means saving fabric and makes the quilt easier to handle.
- Choose a backing layout that best suits your quilt. Note: large quilts might require 3 lengths.

binding

find a video tutorial at: www.msqc.co/006

- Use 2½" strips for binding.
- Sew strips together end-to-end into one long strip using diagonal seams, a.k.a. plus sign method (next). Press seams open.
- Fold in half lengthwise with wrong sides together and press.
- The entire length should equal the outside dimension of the quilt plus 15" - 20".

plus sign method

find a video tutorial at: www.msqc.co/001

- Lay one strip across the other as if to make a plus sign right sides together.
- Sew from top inside to bottom outside corners crossing the intersections of fabric as you sew. Trim the excess fabric ¼" away from the sewn seam.
- Press seam(s) open.

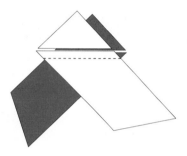

attach binding

- Match raw edges of the folded binding to one edge of the top of the quilt.
- Leave a 10" tail at the beginning.
- Use a ¼" seam allowance.
- Start sewing in the middle of a long straight side.

miter corners

- Stop sewing ¼" before the corner.
- Move the quilt out from under the presser foot.
- Flip the binding up at a 90° angle to the edge just sewn.
- Fold the binding down along the next side to be sewn, aligning raw edges.
- The fold will lie along the edge just completed.
- Begin sewing on the fold.

close binding

- Stop sewing when you have 12" left to reach the start.
- Where the binding tails come together, trim excess leaving only 2½" of overlap.
- Pin or clip the quilt together at the two points where the binding starts and stops to take the pressure off of the binding tails.
- Use the plus sign method to sew the two binding ends together, except this time, match the edges. Using a pencil, mark your sewing line and stitch.
- Trim off excess; press the seam open.
- Fold in half with wrong sides together and align all raw edges to the quilt top.
- Sew this last binding section to the quilt. Press.
- Turn the folded edge of the binding around to the back of the quilt and tack in place with an invisible stitch or machine stitch.

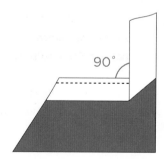

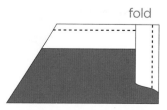